The Family Book of Halloween Fun

The Family Book of Halloween Fun

Joanne O'Sullivan, Vicki Rhodes, Jill Williams Grover,
Shauna Mooney Kawasaki, and Cindy Fuller

Barnes & Noble Books
New York

Library of Congress Cataloging-in-Publication Data Available

10 9 8 7 6 5 4 3 2 1

Material in this collection was adapted from:
Halloween, by Joanne O'Sullivan, © 2003, Lark Books
Pumpkin Decorating, by Vicki Rhodes, © 1997, Chapelle Ltd.
Scary Scenes for Halloween, by Jill Williams Grover, © 1999, Chapelle Ltd.
Ghostly Frights for Halloween Nights, by Shauna Mooney Kawasaki, © 2001, Shauna Mooney Kawasaki
Haunt Your House for Halloween, by Cindy Fuller, © 1997, Chapelle Ltd.

The written instructions, photographs, designs, diagrams, and projects in this volume are intended for the personal use of the reader and may be reproduced for that purpose only. Any other use, especially commercial use, is forbidden under law without the written permission of the copyright holder. Every effort has been made to ensure that all information in this book is accurate. However, due to differing conditions, tools, and individual skills, the publisher cannot be responsible for any injuries, losses, and /or other damages which may result from the use of the information in this book.

Edited by Christine Byrnes
Book design by Liz Trovato
Cover design by Alan Carr

Published by Sterling Publishing Co., Inc.
387 Park Avenue South, New York, NY 10016

Printed in China

ISBN 0-7607-5935-9

Contents

Introduction

When you were a kid, it was all about the candy. Years later, you can still remember the excitement of getting your favorite chocolate bar in spades, and the bitter disappointment of discovering that, once again, your neighbors were giving out nothing but those inferior-quality taffy things. You may have created elaborate cataloguing systems for your candy—chocolates under the bed, lollipops in your sock drawer—or a byzantine barter system with your siblings—four dark chocolate miniatures in exchange for amnesty from a day's chores.

Now that you're a grown-up, you can buy your own candy—as much as you want, whenever you want. So why is Halloween still your favorite holiday? Maybe it's because Halloween puts us in touch with the magical—something that's notably absent in our sensible grown-up lives. As the sun goes down and the chilly fall wind whips leaves around in an eerie dance, even the most level-headed adults must admit that there's something in the air on Halloween night, a ghost of a chance that there may be, well, a ghost or two hovering about. Perhaps it's because on this night, even a grown-up can break free from a polished appearance and a poised demeanor to become, for just one night, an enchanted being, a terrifying beast, or a sultry sorceress. Or maybe it's because Halloween is the one holiday that's all about fun, pure and simple. There are no presents to buy, no stressful family dynamics to deal with, no giant dinner to cook—just playing dress-up, and enjoying time with friends.

Since kids and grown-ups love Halloween for different reasons, we thought it was about time there was a Halloween guide with a decidedly adult approach to the holiday. The family can all participate in these activities, making Halloween a family holiday with a grown up style. Dress up or deck the halls in orange and black. Hold a fabulous fête that will keep your friends talking until New Year's Eve. We've got all the ideas you need right here.

Halloween is almost here. Tap into the magic that's in the air and celebrate this bewitching holiday with a kid's enthusiasm and a grown up's sense of style.

than scare them, ghosts were depicted as friendly, and jack-o'lanterns had smiling faces. When the cultural tide turned again in the 1970s, children were warned of the possible dangers in their candy bags. Rumors of contaminated candy circulated, and although they were later proven false, parents no longer felt safe sending their children to their neighbors' doors. Fundamentalist Christian groups decried Halloween as a devil-worshiping holiday and started a campaign to outlaw it. At the same time, Hollywood started churning out "slashers" which promoted the idea of Halloween as a dangerous time when deranged humans, not spirits, roam the streets with murderous intent.

As the cultural pendulum slowly swings back again, Halloween has once again become a holiday celebrated by both children and adults. It has begun to move back across the Atlantic to the countries of its origin in a new form and has crossed the U. S. borders into Mexico and Canada. It's anybody's guess how this holiday will be reinvented as it spreads to other cultures and is discovered by new generations.

Costumes

Our busy grown-up lives offer very few opportunities to act against type. And then, once a year, Halloween night comes along, and all bets are off. You've got carte blanche to be anyone or anything. You want to look creative. You want to look great. And you've only got one night, so you'd better make it good.

If you're usually serious, be outrageous. If you're usually cheerful, be scary. Be what no one would ever expect. We offer ideas beyond the plastic, packaged costumes you find in stores. After all, your costume reflects who you are. Do you really want to be something that came out of the bargain bin?

Peruse the ideas in the following section.

Be inspired.

Black Widow Spider

For a really scary Halloween evening, be an eight-legged enchantress in this black widow spider costume. When your date picks you up, recite interesting facts about the black widow. Note that black widows are the most venomous spiders in North America and that females are usually shy, nocturnal creatures that don't like to leave their webs. Mention that it is true that females do eat their mates after mating, but that if they are well fed, they will allow their mate to live for another day. This should score you dinner at a nice restaurant. Along with your four-legged "spiderpack" wear a black leotard, tights, hat, and gloves.

Materials:

Foam pipe insulation tubes*
Scissors
Black faux fur
Medium-weight cardboard
Black velveteen
Hot glue gun and glue sticks
Heavy-gauge wire
Wire cutter
Work gloves
Cotton or polyester fiberfill
Black elastic banding
Plastic ornament balls**
Strong, soft black yarn
Red craft felt

**Available at hardware stores*
***Available at craft stores*

For the Spider Legs

1. The legs on your "spiderpack" are made from foam insulation tubing. It's lightweight so it won't hurt your back to wear them, and it's usually sold in several lengths. We used two 6-foot (1.8 m) lengths and cut them in half to make four 3-foot-long (91.4 cm) legs.

2. Cut black faux fur covers for the foam legs. Hold a piece of the fur around one leg to determine how much you'll need to cover it. Hot-glue the fabric to the tube, stuffing any extra fur into the hollow tube. Cut a small round cover for one end of the tube and leave the other end open. Repeat for the other tube legs.

3. Cut an oblong piece of cardboard to fit on the center of your back (this is the frame for your spiderpack). Cut a piece of faux fur to the same size, adding a 1-inch (2.5 cm) border all around and set this piece aside.

4. Cut a piece of velveteen material about the same shape as the cardboard piece, but with a 6-inch (15.2 cm) border all around. This piece will be the hump of your spiderpack.

5. Cut two long pieces of the heavy-gauge wire, each just under the length of your arm's span. The wire will serve as the structural support for your furry legs and will be attached to the cardboard shape. Decide where you'd like the legs to be positioned on your back.

6. Wearing work gloves to protect your hands, poke the wire through the cardboard near the edge, then pull it across back of the shape and out through the other side.

7. Make four holes in the large velveteen fabric hump piece, near the edges. Pull the wire through these holes, so that four pieces of wire stick out, positioned to hold the weight of the legs.

8. Hot glue the velveteen hump piece to the back side of the cardboard, leaving an opening so you can insert the stuffing.

9. Stuff the hump with fiberfill, pushing it in until you have a plump pillow shape. Add extra stuffing around the wires so that they don't cut into your back.

10. Hot-glue the round furry piece that you cut in step 3 to the exposed back piece of cardboard.

11. Attach the furry legs to the pack by sliding a leg down each wire. You can bend the wire for better spider leg positions. Attach the legs to the pack with hot-glue so that they are securely in place and don't slide off.

12. Cut two elastic straps to reach from the top of your spiderpack, around your shoulder, and down to the bottom of pack. Attach these straps as though you were preparing a backpack. The top of the straps will be positioned on the spider back so that the straps sit between your shoulder blades. They will reach around your shoulders and attach to the bottom of back close together, near the bottom of your spine. Hot-glue the straps to the pack and sew over them for extra strength if you can.

13. The spider eyes are made from plastic ornament balls, made for sewing craft projects. The mesh pattern on the surface of the balls is wide enough so that you can see through it. Pull the balls apart and spray paint each side whatever color you imagine the eyes to be (red is very striking). Tie a piece of yarn through one of the mesh holes on each side of the ball. Position each side over one of your eyes to find out how long the center piece of yarn (that will go over your nose) should be. Once you've determined a length, thread the yarn through the half-sphere, making little knots inside. Add two long pieces of yarn on the sides to pull back and tie at the back of your head.

14. Cut a red hourglass shape from felt and attach it to your leotard with masking tape.

Dancing Queen

You can dance, you can jive. Have the time of your life. You are the dancing queen. Even if you're no longer young, sweet, or 17, on Halloween night, the ABBA fairy waves her magic wand and gives everyone a chance to be the dancing queen.

This dazzling disco fantasy costume is a piece of cake to make. Gather a pile of free software CDs, starting with the ones you're constantly getting in the mail, then begging for more from your office IT person, who will probably be more than willing to part with them.

Drill a hole in each side of each CD (the holes should be roughly at 12 o'clock, 3 o'clock, 6 o'clock, and 9 o'clock). String the CDs together with thin, clear, plastic cord (obviously you will have made sure that it fits through the holes). For our costume, we used three rows of seven CDs each for the front and two rows of five CDs each for the back (even the dancing queen has to sit down sometimes, so we left off the back middle panel). Tie your two back panels together with a piece of cord running across your back.

Wear all white under your CD dress. Spray paint a pair of boots silver for footwear. Wear disco ball earrings and carry a tambourine. If you've got a date for Halloween night, suggest a Fernando costume so you can be the all-ABBA twosome.

Samurai Warrior

If you're really a fraidy cat in your day-to-day life, Halloween is your chance to be a fearless warrior, like a samurai. This costume is made mostly of joss paper, a specialty Asian paper used to roll incense. You can find heaps of it in any Asian grocery store, and it's quite inexpensive. In the center of each piece of joss paper is a shiny square of metallic leaf, either silver or gold. Pieced together, it looks like panels of samurai armor. If you don't have access to joss paper, try spray painting cardboard silver to achieve the same look.

Materials:

Joss paper*
Scissors
Stapler and staples
Ribbon or 1/2-inch (1.3 cm) wide bias tape
Poster board
Spray adhesive
Aluminum flashing
Ballpoint pen
Black baseball cap
Hot glue gun and glue sticks

**Sold in large, inexpensive packets at Asian grocery stores*

For the Skirt

1. Start with the long panel that hangs down the center front of the costume. You'll need to trim the plain borders of the joss paper to about 1/2 inch (1.3 cm) from the metallic square in the center. This panel uses seven pieces of paper, but you may use more or less depending on your height.

2. Start stapling together the pieces on the long center panel. You'll be stapling all the pieces together vertically, like in figure 1. You'll need to start with the bottom square and staple along the top of the squares so that you can hide the staples under the next layer you add.

3. When you've got the center panel done, you can start on the rest of the panels for the skirt. The number of panels you need and their length is dependent on your width and height. For this skirt, we used six panels of five squares each. Each vertical panel is stapled together with the same process used in step 2.

4. Lay all the panels on a flat surface with the long center panel in the middle. Start stapling the panels together by overlapping them. The top square of each panel should be stapled to the adjacent square in the center so that the staples are hidden by the overlap. The rest of the squares can hang loose.

5. Once all the top squares are stapled together, staple a black ribbon horizontally across the top squares to serve as a belt. Make sure it's long enough to fit around your waist and tie.

6. Staple a series of squares over the black ribbon to hide it.

For the Chest Piece

1. Lay out the pieces of paper in the shape shown in figure 3. Starting at the bottom, staple them together so that the staples stay hidden.

2. To add strength at the shoulder area, attach the squares to the poster board with spray adhesive before you staple them to the top of the chest piece.

3. Cut two pieces of ribbon and staple one piece to each shoulder. Make it long enough to tie in back or loop under your arms and tie in front.

4. Cover the ribbon on the shoulder area by adding two additional squares of joss paper.

For the Hat

Draw the samurai emblem on a piece of aluminum flashing and cut it out carefully with scissors. Cut out additional aluminum circles and hot-glue them to the bill of the black baseball cap. Glue the emblem to the bill of the cap with the hot glue gun. Accordion pleat six pieces of joss paper and staple four of the pieces to the side edge of the cap and the two remaining pieces above them on the cap

See below for instructions on making the sword.

En Garde! Weapons & Armaments

Besides making a costume scarier, weapons make a costume, well, more manly. It's a rare man who will venture into a craft store in search of costume materials. Men can find the materials for these weapons where they live—in the building materials department of a home improvement store. They're all made from aluminum flashing—the stuff used around gutters and on roofs. It's flexible, easy to cut, and looks a lot more like real metal than that fake plastic stuff used to make store-bought costume weapons.

You can make weapons to accessorize any kind of costume from any period of time. Just take a look at historical images in books or on-line to figure out the design for your armaments. When you've got a design in mind, just trace it onto a piece of flashing and cut it out with scissors.

If the edges are too sharp and you're worried about actually harming someone, bind the sides with metal repair tape (which can also be found at home improvement or hardware stores and blends very well with flashing). To make your arms sturdier, it's best to cut out two identical pieces and hot glue them together.

The axe above is a great complement to a Viking costume. The axe shape is attached to a piece of black plastic piping with black electrical tape. The piping is lightweight, and like the other materials, it lives in home improvement stores.

An aluminum flashing scythe(in photo, above) is made by the same process and, of course, is the must-have accouterment for the grim reaper.

To give interest to this sword and make it sturdier, you can run a ballpoint pen down the center, causing it to fold and creating contours. Depending on the shape you choose, this sword could be used with a gladiator (page 21) or samurai costume (page 16).

Men of war need to protect themselves from blows to the head, so you'll need a helmet, too. The Viking-inspired helmet above is made from strips of aluminum flashing fitted to the wearer's head and held together with silver duct tape (or metal repair tape). Two bands cross on top of the head and attach to the central band that wraps around the head. To mimic the embellishments on a real Viking helmet, flat back marbles (all right, you probably do need to go to a craft store for those) were spray painted sliver and hot glued to the bands. Lush faux fur is duct taped in between the cross bands on the top to finish it off.

The mace that you see accompanying the helmet is made from a doggie chew toy spray painted silver, attached to a chain, and duct taped to a spraypainted dowel. Very intimidating.

Faux Fur Fifi, the French Poodle

Ooo-la-la! If you wear this costume to a contest, you're bound to get "Best in Show." Fifi has come straight from the doggie beauty parlor with a fresh haircut and she's ready to show it off. Along with a dog collar, you'll need to accessorize this costume with a lot of attitude. Paint a snout and whiskers on your face, and get ready to be the center of attention.

Materials:

White body suit
Upholstery foam*
Scissors
Faux fur
Medium-gauge wire
Wire cutters or pliers
Cotton or polyester fiberfill
Needle and strong invisible thread or fishing line
Hot glue gun and glue sticks (optional)
Knit cap
Gloves or mittens
Slippers
Dog collar
**Available at fabric stores*

1. Start with the tail, which is the only piece that needs to be attached to the bodysuit. Cut a cylindrical shape from the foam. It should be about 2 to 3 inches (5.1 to 7.6 cm) long and about $1\frac{1}{2}$-inches (3.2 cm) wide.

2. Cut a piece of wire about 6 inches (15.2 cm) longer than the foam cylinder. Poke the wire through the middle of the foam, allowing it to extend out on both ends. On one end, bend the wire into a spiral, and hot-glue it to the bodysuit in the appropriate position (you may need to try the bodysuit on and mark the spot). Roll a small tuft of faux fur into a ball (tucking it under and gluing it in place if necessary), and hot glue it to the other end of the wire.

3. To make the poodle "vest," measure from your shoulders to just below your rib cage, then double that measurement, and cut a piece of faux fur to that size (use one of your everyday shirts as a guide for determining the width). Fold the piece in half and cut an opening for your head in the center of the fold line. Pull the piece over your head and figure out where you need to bind up the sides for a tight but comfortable fit. Mark where the bottom of your arm openings should be and any places where you need to cut off excess fabric for a smooth fit.

4. Hand stitch the sides of the vest closed with strong thread or fishing line. You could also hot-glue the sides closed if you're not comfortable with sewing.

5. Wrap a piece of fur around your wrist to get the approximate length and width measurement. The fur should fit snugly, but you've got to be able to get the tuft over your hand. Follow the same process to decide on the measurements for the ankle tufts. When you're satisfied with the measurements, cut the tufts. They should resemble oversized, puffy arm tufts and leg warmers.

6. Sew or hot-glue the long edges of the tufts together. Stuff a little fiberfill into the tube you created, then stitch or glue the two short sides together to form a ring.

7. The thigh tufts are constructed like the wrist and ankle tufts. Fit them to your thighs, making sure they're tight enough to stay in place. Sew or glue the long edges together. When stuffing the tufts, however, don't overstuff. Otherwise your thigh tufts will rub together, making it difficult to walk. When you're finished stuffing, sew or hot-glue the short ends closed to form a ring. If you find it easier, and less restrictive, you can glue all the tufts into place on the bodysuit, although the vest will certainly have to come over your head as a separate piece.

8. The cap serves as a base for the head and ears. For the ears, simply cut an ear shape from fur that will be draped over the top of your head. They should be long enough to hang past your jaw line and can be lined with pink faux fur if you wish (cut the pink fur to the same size as the ears and glue the two pieces wrong sides together). Hot-glue or sew the top of the ears to the top of the cap.

9. Ball up a bunch of fur (similar to the tail ball, only larger) to serve as a head tuft. Glue or sew the tuft to the front of the cap.

10. When you put on your tufts, be sure that the seams fall on the inside of your arms and legs where you will not see them. As a finishing touch, add a dog collar and slippers in a color to match the rest of your ensemble. You can paint paws onto them with fabric paint if you like. Finis!

Gladiator

If you've got a nice pair of legs, show them off with this gladiator costume. If you're more skilled with a sword than a sewing machine, not to worry. This is a no-sew costume, held together mostly with hot glue. Make sure you wear something underneath, as the "skirt" on the bottom is too revealing even for the most ardent exhibitionist.

Materials:

Measuring tape
Brown vinyl, about 2 yards (1.8 m)
Marker
Scissors
Brown spray paint (optional)
Aluminum flashing
Hot glue gun and glue sticks
Awl or ice pick
Leather cord

For the Skirt

1. Measure, mark, and cut a piece of brown vinyl for the skirt. You'll want the piece to fit around your waist and to right about your knees. If the underside of the vinyl is white, then spray paint it brown so that it blends.

2. Measure and mark in two spots: about 4 inches (10.2 cm) in and 2 inches (5.1 cm) down from one long edge of the vinyl. Starting at the opposite long edge, cut up to the mark to create a loose strip. Continue cutting strips vertically up the fabric this way to create the skirt's fringe.

When you get to the center of the fabric, make a few of the strips a bit thinner.

3. Cut 2 inches (5.1 cm) off the bottom of all of the strips except thinner strips in the front middle. Trim the rest of the strips into a point at the bottom.

4. Cut small squares from the aluminum flashing (make sure they're not too big to fit on the strips of the skirt). Hot-glue them to the strips (except for the long thin ones in the front).

5. Cut aluminum flashing circles to fit on the thin front strips, then glue them to the strips.

6. Poke holes with an awl or ice pick at the top back of the skirt and thread leather cord through the holes to lace the skirt closed.

For the Shirt

1. Start the shirt by cutting four pieces of vinyl, each long enough to fit comfortably around your mid-section and about 5 inches (12.7 cm) wide. Hot-glue the strips together on the long edges to form a tiered, layered piece.

2. Fold a piece of vinyl in half and figure out how big a piece you'll need to create a neck piece that reaches from just over your ribs, over your shoulders, then down to the end of your shoulder blades. Cut a piece to this width, then shape the sides of the fabric as you see in the picture on page 21. Hot-glue the four-layered piece to the bottom of this neckpiece.

3. Cut four pieces of vinyl to attach to the edge of the neckpiece as sleeves. The pieces should just cover your shoulders and flare out a bit. Hot-glue two pieces to each other as a cap sleeve, then hot glue the sleeve to the edge of the neckpiece. Repeat for the other side.

4. Cut an opening through the front center of the top so that you can get into it. Cut narrow strips of vinyl and hot-glue one end of each strip to one side of the opening you cut.

5. Use an awl or ice pick to poke a hole in the unattached end of each strip you cut. Poke a corresponding hole in the shirt, right under the hole you poked in the narrow strip. Cut a piece of leather cord for each strip and lace it through the holes to hold the shirt closed.

6. Decorate the edges of the neckpiece with little cut squares of aluminum flashing attached with hot glue.

Accessories

Sandals

Wear regular sandals and wrap long strips of vinyl up your calves to imitate Roman sandals. Tape the ends of the vinyl together to keep the straps in place.

Sword

See page 17 for instructions.

Shield

The shield is made from a silver party platter. The ornament in the middle is a curtain tieback hot glued to the platter. The gold nail design is made from flat-backed marbles spray painted gold and hot glued to the platter. Create a strap on the back with a piece of duct tape. Lay two pieces of duct tape (one longer than the other) together, centering the shorter one on top of the larger one, sticky sides together. Attach the sticky part that didn't get covered to the back of the platter.

Winged Things

For filmy wings fit for a fairy or any other magical winged creature, try this technique. The diaphanous look is achieved with iridescent wrapping paper that's laminated in a pouch laminator. These wings are as light as air and catch the light as you flit through the room.

Materials:

Large piece of poster board
Marker
1 yard (91.4 cm) of iridescent cellophane wrapping paper
Scissors
11 x 17-inch (27.9 x 43.2 cm) pouch laminator*
26-gauge silver floral wire
Straight pins
Sewing machine with heavyweight needle
Needle and invisible thread (optional)
**Available at copy service centers*

1. Refer to pictures of dragonflies or fairies to decide on the shape for your wings. Remember that each wing will need to fit inside the 11 x 17-inch (27.9 x 43.2 cm) laminator, so be sure to make each wing smaller than that. Draw each wing separately on a piece of poster board to make templates.

2. Crinkle the iridescent wrapping paper into a ball and then flatten it back out.

3. Use the template as a guide to cut each wing shape separately from the wrapping paper. Cut them slightly smaller than the template size so you'll have a 1/4-inch (6 mm) laminate border after you run the wings through the laminator.

4. Take the wings to the nearest pouch laminator (if you have one at work, all the better) and carefully lay one of the wings inside it.

5. Use floral wire to make the veins in the wings. Just cut it into pieces to fit on top of the wing and position them in a vein pattern.

6. Send the wing through the laminator. Repeat the process for the other wing.

7. Trim the excess lamination from around the wing, leaving just a small border around the cellophane wing.

8. Put on your costume and have a friend pin the wings to the back of it with the straight pins. Stitch the wings onto the costume using a basting stitch on the sewing machine or hand sew them in position.

Variation

If you'd prefer to be a bee, or a ladybug, or a fly on the wall, use black plastic mesh screening (used for screen doors and windows) over an iridescent cellophane wing to imitate the texture of insect wings.

After you cut your wing template, use it to create one set of wings from cellophane and two sets from plastic mesh screen. Sandwich the iridescent wing piece between the two layers of the mesh wings. Create a wing shape from 20-gauge floral wire, attached end-to-end and reinforced with floral tape. Bind the layers (mesh, wire, wrapping paper, mesh) of each wing together with electrical tape, or hot glue and bias tape. Use a strong wire to connect the wings, making sure that they're at least a finger's breadth apart.

Attach a ribbon to the strong wire in the center of the wings to act as a harness that you'll run over your shoulders and under your arms. Adjust the wings on your back so that they sit where you want them to, and safety pin the ribbon to the rest of your costume so that the wings don't move. If you choose not to use a harness for the wings, you can simply stitch or safety pin them directly onto your costume.

Frothy Fairy Frock & Headpiece

Since few people have ever actually seen a fairy, you have creative license to wear whatever you want when impersonating one for Halloween. The lovely layered effect you see in this dress is achieved by spray painting through a piece of lace, then adding layers of tulle on top. Sprinkle everything with a heaping helping of fairy dust (also known as glitter) so that you'll sparkle when you catch the light. Top your frock with a sparkly crown-like headpiece, and don't forget the wings on page 23.

Materials:

Slip or nightgown
Doily
Piece of scrap lace or curtain
Silver spray paint
Stapler and staples
White tulle
Safety pins
Ribbon or colored tulle
Sequins or rhinestones
Hot glue gun and glue sticks
Glitter
Piece of pliable woody vine, such as grapevine
Florist wire or thin gauge craft wire
Wire snips
Beads or buttons
Scissors
Silver ribbon

1. Place the slip on a flat surface. Lay a piece of lace or a doily on top of it and spray paint through the lace to create a lace stencil. Let dry.

2. Staple a strip of lace (that you haven't painted through) around the bottom of the slip to make it ankle length.

3. Pin the tulle around the bottom edge of the bra area, including the back, to form a layer over the skirt of the slip.

4. Hot glue ribbon or colored tulle over the safety pins to hide them.

5. Hot-glue sequins or rhinestones in a pattern of your choice in the bra area of the slip and on the tulle overlayer. Sprinkle glitter over the entire costume.

For the Headpiece

1. Hold a piece of grapevine to your head and cut it to fit your head. Twist the vine into a circle.

2. Using the wire snips, cut a piece of the floral wire about the same length as the vine. Wrap the wire around the vine several times to make sure it doesn't unwind.

3. Cut several 1-yard (91.4 cm) pieces of floral wire. Wrap one wire a few times around the headpiece and then leave about 1 inch (2.5 cm) of wire sticking up. Thread beads or buttons onto the wire, then make a knot in the wire to secure the embellishment, and loop it back down onto the headpiece, wrapping it around several times to secure it. Continue adding embellishments in this manner. For variety, stagger the height of the embellished loops or bend them in opposing directions.

4. Wrap silver ribbon around the headpiece and tie it at the back. Add a few more pieces of silver ribbon to flow down from the headpiece to the back of the neck.

Shimmery Mermaid

If you want to be a magical enchantress for Halloween, you've got to choose between the dark side and the light. If black magic is more to your taste, there are any number of evil temptresses to imitate. If you gravitate toward more positive energy, a mermaid is an excellent choice. Creating a fishtail that still allows for movement of human legs is always a challenge. This solution uses a tight-fitting skirt and a cast-off pair of athletic shorts as a base.

The top is the answer to a modest mermaid lover's prayers. No seashell bikini tops here. The shells are decorative wooden ornaments attached to a green slip that will keep you from shivering too much on a cold October night.

Materials:

Several green fabric remnants in different textures, preferably shimmery
Scissors
Tight-fitting skirt
Baggy, elastic-waist athletic shorts
Hot glue gun and glue sticks
Gold elastic sequin trim
Decorative wooden shell shapes or craft foam shells*
Shell jewelry or faux pearls

**Used for embellishing mantelpieces or wooden borders in homes, these can be found in home improvement stores. Craft foam shells can be found at craft stores.*

1. Find several different kinds of green fabrics that remind you of mermaids. You can use inexpensive fabric remnants from a fabric store or cut up old clothing that you no longer use. Cut a fish-scale shape from each of the fabrics (long, flat on one side, curved on the other). Use your first scale as a template to create others. Depending on your size, you may need several dozen scales in each fabric. This is a great project to do while you're doing something else like talking on the phone or watching TV.

2. For the base, use a skirt that's a thrift store find or cast-off in a green or shimmery aqua-colored fabric. Since you won't see much of the skirt under the scales, it's OK if it's damaged. The skirt should be tight fitting, preferably made of a stretchy synthetic material, and should reach to mid-calve length. Lay the skirt on a flat surface and, starting at the waistband, hot glue the scales to the skirt (you can sew them on if you know how). Layer the scales like roof shingles so that very little of the original skirt shows through. When you get to the bottom of the skirt, let the scales hang over the edge a little as a fringe.

3. The tail (made from the athletic shorts) will flair out from underneath the skirt. You can cut open the outside of the shorts so that the material drags enough to hide your feet, and cut open the inside so that your legs are hidden The shorts should appear to split in the middle and come to two points at your feet. Stretch out the elastic waist of the shorts and hot-glue the top of shorts to the bottom edge of the skirt so that the overlapping scales hide the top. You should only apply the glue in a few places rather than all around so that the shorts will drape more loosely around your ankles.

4. Hot-glue sequin trim to the top of the skirt at the waistband to distinguish your human half from your fish tail. You can also add it on the bottom of the tail.

5. For your human half, use a tank top, slip, or even a long-sleeved green shirt that can be tucked inside the skirt. Hot-glue two thin wooden shell shapes or craft foam shells to the shirt in the appropriate place.

6. Shell jewelry or faux pearls with shells glued on and draped around your neck will add the finishing touches. Wear flip-flops, green socks, or no shoes at all.

Queen Bee & Drone

Looking for a sure-fire way to create a buzz at any Halloween party? Find a willing drone and go as the Queen Bee. Here's a quick review of beehive politics: the queen bee has thousands of drones at her disposal, flying around and collecting nectar as she sits regally on her throne back at the hive laying thousands of eggs. The young, willing drones live only to mate with the queen and then die immediately after doing so. This is the perfect costume to wear if you're commitment-shy and want to get the message across to your date.

Materials:

Yellow electrical tape
Black clothing for top and bottom
Scissors
Black deer netting
Black stretch belt
Stapler and staples
Black spray paint
Aluminum flashing
Ballpoint pen
Metal repair tape or duct tape
Landscape fabric
Needle and thread
Polyester fiberfill
Safety pins

Both the queen and the drone will tape strips of yellow electrical tape to their clothing. The queen looks best in a leotard with tights underneath, while the drone can get away with wearing a black turtleneck or sweatshirt and some jeans (he is a worker, after all). The drone then needs only to add a tool belt, some boots, and some sort of antennae—this one is a fur-covered headband with a black pipe cleaner wrapped around it. For the insect wings, see instructions on page 21.

The queen's costume is a little more detailed. For the skirt, cut deer netting to the desired length, then staple it to a black belt. We added several layers, pleated for fullness. You can spray paint the staples black to hide them.

The crown is made from aluminum flashing, which you'll fit to your head. Just draw a honeycomb pattern on the flashing with a pen or marker and cut out the center inside the pattern. Tape the crown closed at the back with metal repair tape or duct tape.

To make the stinger, cut two triangular pieces of the landscape fabric. Sew or staple the pieces together wrong side out, leaving a small opening so that you can stuff the stinger. Turn it right side out and stuff it with fiberfill, then fold over the open edges and safety pin them in place. Staple the stinger to the top of the belt.

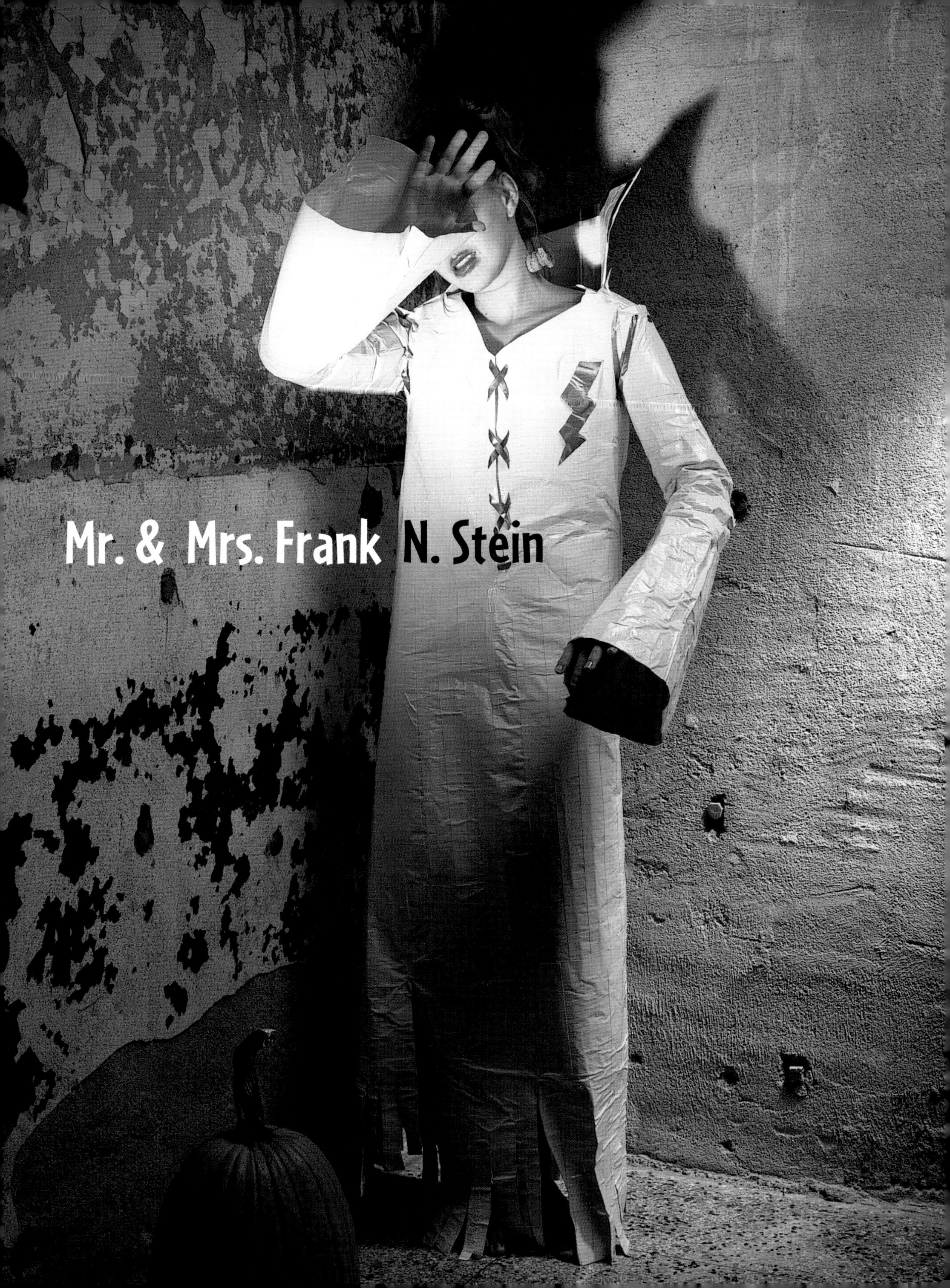

Mr. & Mrs. Frank N. Stein

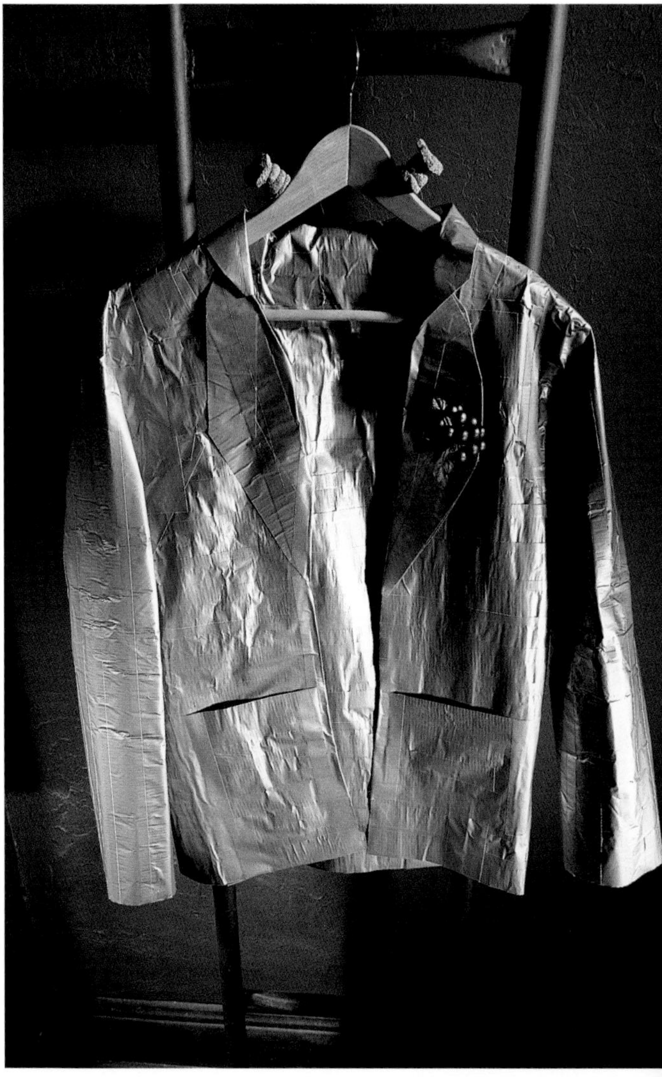

If Frankenstein's monster and his mate were created today, they wouldn't be caught undead in anything but duct tape clothing.

A few years back, underground fashionistas started making wallets and handbags from duct tape, and the trend quickly spread. Soon high school students were making all kinds of clothing from this humble but durable material. Duct tape clothing has become all the rage at prom time thanks to a national contest with big cash prizes sponsored by a prominent duct tape company.

Materials:

Duct tape
Scissors
Cardboard (optional)
Upholstery foam
Fishing line or clear thread
Large-eye needle
Gray paint
Small paintbrush
Clear elastic cord

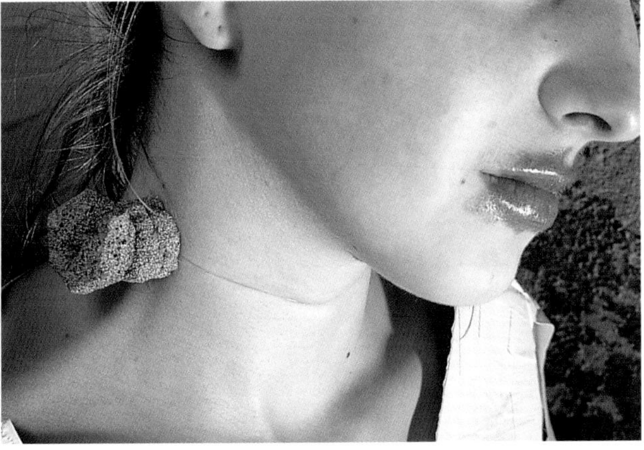

For the Dress

1. Start with a strip of duct tape that runs from your shoulder to ankle (or whatever length you want the dress to be). Place the strip (adhesive side up) on the floor, and cut another piece of the same length. Line up the outside edges of the two pieces and press the adhesive side of each together. This forms a strip with two smooth sides and no sticky mess.

2. Take another strip of the same length and lay one-third of this piece over the first piece. Then back this with a fourth piece of the same length.

3. Continue the process of overlapping and backing until the strips form a sheet of duct tape that is big enough to go from one side of you to the other. Repeat the same process to build the back half of the dress.

4. When you've built both sides of the dress, cut the two panels into the shape you want (curved in above the hips, flared at the bottom, etc.).

5. To join the two panels, just line up the sides and position a piece of duct tape (sticky side down) overlapping each panel. Repeat this process until the sides are joined, then repeat it on the other side.

6. To add the sleeves, build two panels just like the ones you built to make the front and back of the dress. Wrap one of the panels around your arm and tape it together to fit, then repeat this process for the other sleeve.

7. To attach the sleeves to the dress, cut holes in the top of the sleeves and corresponding holes in the shoulders of the dress. Lace the sleeves to the dress with a thin strip of duct tape.

8. Cut a slit down one of the sides from the underarm almost to the bottom of the dress. Put a strip of hook-and-loop fastener tape on each side inside the slit. Now you can get in and out of the dress.

9. For the neck detail, cut a slit from the neck down to about 4 inches (10.2 cm) above the waist. Cut equally spaced holes on each side of the slit. For the lacing, take a long piece of duct tape and fold it in half so that the sticky side folds back on itself. Lace this strip up through the holes.

10. To make the collar, cut a cardboard rectangle with a flared top, and cover it (front and back) with duct tape. Tape the collar to the outside of the neck.

For the Neck Bolts

1. Cut two pieces of upholstery foam into 1 x 2-inch (2.5 x 5.1 cm) cylinders.

2. Cut two more pieces into hexagon shapes, each with a 1-inch (2.5 cm) diameter. Each hexagon should be about ½-inch (1.3 cm) thick.

3. Sew the hexagon to the cylinder with a large-eyed needle and piece of fishing line.

4. Wrap fishing line around the cylinder to squeeze it into a bolt shape. Paint the whole piece gray and let dry.

5. Poke a hole through the end of each bolt with the needle and thread a piece of elastic through the hole. Fit the bolts to your neck and tie the elastic in back when you've got the right fit.

For the Jacket

Follow the same overlapping process you used to make the dress, except that the sleeves are attached directly to the jacket.

Mother Nature & the Green Man

Peeking out of the leaves in the forest are two mysterious figures swathed in green. Are they human, supernatural, or a little bit of both? This costumed couple consists of Mother Nature, the all-powerful source of life on earth, and the Green Man, the enigmatic medieval archetype of the woods whose leafy face is fascinating but a little frightening. If you and your party companion are friends of the earth, this is the most enviro-friendly couples' costume you can create.

What's the fuzzy green stuff they're both wearing? It's a natural fiber material designed to line the bottom of hanging baskets and flowerbeds to encourage growth and keep out weeds. It looks fantastic and is the perfect material for this costume, but we won't lie to you—it's itchy and it sheds. You must wear something under your costume if you use it, and you'll definitely have to vacuum your floor later (it's best to assemble this in the garage or basement).

This is one of those one-night-only materials. The good news is that as you prepare your garden for next spring, you need only lay your costume down in the soil and let Mother Nature work her magic. If you can't find this marvelous material, try using green felt instead or dye a piece of white faux fur green.

Mother Nature

Mother Nature wears a green shirt that's been embellished with an array of fake natural elements—silk flowers, leaves, vines, butterflies, stuffed birds, and plastic berries. All the greenery is cut from craft store finds and hot glued to the shirt. The birds come with wires attached to their legs, so the wires were poked through the shirt and twisted shut.

The skirt is simply two pieces of fiber basket liner cut in a flared-skirt shape. To attach the pieces, we poked holes along the sides of each piece with an awl and laced the sides together with leather cord, knotting it at the bottom. We cut a few slits along the top to thread an adjustable belt through. More vines, birds, and leaves grace Mother Nature's skirt, kept in place with hot glue.

Now for the pièce de résistance—the hat. The base is simply an old hat from a thrift store. We hot glued silk leaves over it to cover it up, then hot glued the nest on top (you can find these nests at any craft store). Add birds (cardinals are nice and colorful), bird's eggs, and silk flowers to make it more inviting. Wildlife of all kinds will flock to Mother Nature in this comely costume.

The Green Man

The Green Man's tunic is also made from fiber liner—one long strip folded in half, with a circle cut out at the fold line for the neck hole. Holes for lacing were poked in sides on both the front and back with an awl. Leather cord is laced through the holes to stitch the front and back together, and knotted at the end. A front slit with leather lacing was added at the front for a little more comfort and interest.

The Green Man wears fake vines and oak leaves as well as real birch bark, all attached with hot glue. This modern green man (who's a gardener in real life) wears jeans under his tunic, but any casual pants would be acceptable.

The Green Man's crowing glory is the oak leaf mask, which should be left on at all times! Whatever you do, don't try to make this mask from the fiber liner material. Use craft foam as a base instead. Trace a basic mask shape (page 49) onto a piece of brown or green craft foam. Extend the shape below the eyes down to rest on the cheek, leaving the nose and mouth uncovered. Punch holes on both sides of the mask, level with the eye holes. Hot glue real or artificial leaves (oak leaves look best) to the mask, overlapping them as desired. Thread a doubled length of cord or ribbon through the holes.

Here Comes the Judge

If you never get a chance to pass judgment on people during your daily life, Halloween offers the opportunity. In your judge persona, you can make up creative sentencing for people who wear bad costumes or take the last chocolate chip cookie from the dessert table. If you really want to intimidate people, carry a noose and be a hanging judge.

Then again, how intimidating can you really be with a bunch of toilet paper rolls on your head?

Judge's Robe

The robe is simply a red bed sheet, double-sized. You could also use a big tablecloth or curtain. Simply wrap the sheet around you and discreetly tuck one end under the other. You can safety pin it together if you like.

Judge's Wig

You don't need to start collecting empty paper towel or toilet paper rolls months in advance to make the headpiece. Sending out an e-mail at work should immediately net you dozens of rolls from eco-conscious coworkers who recycle. If you use paper towel rolls, just cut them in half and sand the rough edges a bit.

When you've got enough rolls to make about five long plaits (the four side plaits on this wig used 11 rolls, while the top and center plait used 17), paint them white with craft or spray paint.

To sew your wig together, double thread a large-eye needle with fishing line. Poke a hole through one side of one roll, and pull the needle through to the other side with small pliers. Make a knot and cover it with a drop of cyanoacrylate glue to make sure the line doesn't slip back through the hole. Add another roll to the same piece of fishing line using the same process. Keep going until your plait reaches the length you want. Repeat the threading process on the opposite end of the roll to make it sturdy. After you've got four plaits of equal length, make one that's long enough to go across the top of your head and match the length of the side plaits.

Lay all your plaits on a flat surface with the longer one in the middle. Sew the plaits together, securing each one to the long center plait and adding one loop on the top roll that ties each plait to the one adjacent to it.

Neck & Wrist Ruffles

For the Neck Ruffle

Lay two large coffee filters on top of each other and fold them into a triangle. Repeat for two more sets of coffee filters for a total of three sets of two-layer triangles. Staple the top of the triangles so that the folds stay down. Center one of the triangles on top of another and staple the two together. Make sure you only staple through the first layer rather than all the way through—that way the staples will be hidden. Center the joined triangles on top of the third triangle and staple, again hiding staples. You'll have a staggered look.

Center a piece of ribbon near the top of the top triangle. Fold the point of the triangle over and staple to create a flap. Tie the ribbon around your neck to wear the ruffle. On the front side of the ruffles (the side where you can't see staples), punch holes around the edges of the coffee filters to create a lacey look.

For the Cuffs

Slit four coffee filters on one side and cut the flat center out of them. Stack them on top of each other. Staple white ribbon around the open edge. You can paint over the staples with correction liquid if you want to.

Punch holes around the edges for the lace effect. Repeat the whole process for the second cuff.

Bed Sheet Geisha

You may have seen someone wearing a geisha costume before. Chances are she was wearing a bathrobe. The problem with this costume solution is that instead of looking like you're about to entertain gentlemen in a teahouse, you look as though you're about to brush your teeth and go to bed. Try making a kimono from a sheet instead. You don't need to sew it together, although you can if you know how. Add a geisha mask made from a clip art image (it can serve as a fan, too).

Materials:

1 double flat sheet with contrasting edge
Iron
Scissors
Measuring tape
Fusible webbing (optional)
Sewing machine (optional)
Fray retardant (optional)
1 twin flat sheet
Safety pins

For the Kimono

1. Iron the sheet, then cut off the contrasting edge and set it aside until later.

2. Fold the sheet in half. Locate the center of the fold with a measuring tape and mark the center. Cut out a neck hole at this spot, then cut down the length of the sheet. This will be the front opening of the kimono.

3. Measure 12 inches (30.5 cm) in from each short side of the sheet and cut in a straight line from the edge to this line. Measure 26 inches (66 cm) down from the fold and cut in so that your cut ends at the 12-inch (30.5 cm) mark, cutting off the bottom of the sheet so that you have sleeves.

4. Close up the side seams of the sleeves with the fusible webbing and an iron or the sewing machine.

5. Reattach the contrasting edge over the front opening and neck hole, either with the fusible webbing or sewing machine. It doesn't have to reach the end of the kimono, just to about your knee.

For the Obi

Fold the twin flat sheet lengthwise into a 12-inch (30.5 cm) wide strip and safety pin the edges together. Tie the obi around the back.

Mask instructions on page 42.

Copyright-Free Image Masks

Here's a way to use some of the wonderful pre-existing imagery out there on-line or in books without having to worry about a lawsuit.

Find a copyright-free image. Graphics that are more than 70 years old usually are, but double-check to make sure. Clip art images or engravings taken from books or web sites are good sources. Enlarge the image (you may need to go to a copy shop to get the image as large as you need it for a mask). Mount the image on foam-core board with adhesive spray, then carefully cut around it with a craft knife. Color and embellish it as you wish. Use a flat paint stirring stick as a holder. Decorate your mask as desired (felt-tipped markers work well), then simply glue it to the stick. If you like, you can cut out eye holes. Not only is this an easy on and off mask, it can also be used a fan in a hot, crowded roomful of revelers.

Fetching Flamenca

If you'd rather be alluring than alarming this Halloween, you can't go wrong with a flamenca costume. Delve into the depths of your linen drawer and find an old red tablecloth, or pick one up at a thrift store. Wear a black leotard on top, and if your own hair won't cooperate, add a black wig so your mantilla will have a secure place to sit. A fan is a must-have accessory for flirting provocatively with your admirers. Be prepared to perform Spanish dances on demand.

Materials:

Old red tablecloth, curtain, fabric scrap, or large scarf
Scissors
Red and black crepe paper
Hot glue gun and glue sticks
Lace or doily
Black spray paint
Plastic food container or transparent plastic sheet
Hair comb
Black tulle

1. Wrap the tablecloth or fabric around yourself to make sure it fits. You don't want it to be too tight, as you'll need a little extra fabric for the tie of the skirt. The back should be slightly longer than the front with the longest point in the middle of the back of the skirt.

2. Cut the material into a half circle with two tabs for the ties on the flat edge. Make two small holes in the tabs. You will thread each tab through the hole in the opposite tab to tie the skirt closed.

3. The next step is best done outdoors. Lay the skirt out on a flat surface and lay the lace or doily over it. Spray paint over the lace with black spray paint to create a stenciled lace effect on the red fabric.

4. Glue the first layer of crepe paper around the bottom edge of the skirt with a glue gun, adding two additional layers in contrasting colors as the previous layer dries. Glue only the inner edge of the paper so that the outer edge remains loose to resemble lace.

5. Create the crepe paper sleeve ruffles the same way you made the skirt ruffle—just use short pieces of crepe paper sized to fit your shoulders. You can just tape the ruffles to your shoulders rather than gluing them down so that you can use the leotard later for something else.

6. For the mantilla, cut a rectangle with a slightly flared top from the transparent plastic. The bottom of the rectangle should be the same width as the hair comb.

7. Place the lace or doily over the transparent plastic rectangle and spray paint over it with black spray paint. The lace pattern will be stenciled onto the plastic.

8. Hot-glue the transparent piece onto the comb.

9. Hot-glue a black tulle veil to the back of the comb and arrange the comb in your hair or wig.

Formerly Formal

It all begins with a promise. He and she promise to love each other forever. She promises you, her best friend, will be right there beside her as she takes her vows. Then she promises that you will be able to wear that dress again. Yes, that peach-colored, puffy-sleeved, taffeta dress that makes you look like a circus attraction. You can wear it again, but only as a Halloween costume. First, embrace the fact that there is absolutely nothing you can do to make this dress wearable, except as a costume. Once you've come to terms with that, you will be free to disassemble it and reinterpret it in any way you can dream up.

Before

Three classic bridesmaid or formal styles: the puffy-sleeved with a ribbon in back, the spaghetti strap with an a-line skirt (okay, this one really isn't all that bad) and the empire waist, short puffy sleeves with a draping neckline.

After

It took less than three hours to transform each of these dresses, and none of them required sewing. Turn the page to find out how each dress was reinterpreted.

Dress I

What a difference a spray makes! This dress went from classic 1980s bridal to Queen Elizabeth I. The waistline suggested an Elizabethan style, so the bow was removed and the back became the front. A generous coat of metallic gold spray paint over the entire dress made things better immediately. Upholstery remnants were used for the panels. The pattern on the middle panel and the sleeve additions was made by laying a piece of lace over the top of the fabric and spray painting through it. The sleeves were secured inside the puffs with electrical tape. The stripes on the puffy sleeves were attached with hot glue, as was the fabric panel over the top center. Those little gold crosses are flooring tile spacers spray painted gold. Small faux pearls are hot-glued to the center. A little inexpensive trim was hot-glued along the edges. Finally, we spray painted doilies and taped them inside the sleeves and under the waistline to resemble lace. Add some faux pearls, and you're ready to start crushing the Spanish Armada.

Dress II

Something about the silver of this dress said Marie Antoinette. This design was based very loosely on one of her later portraits. She liked layers and lots of ribbons. The fabric sashes were attached to the dress by poking a thin wire through the dress and twisting it on the inside (you could also sew them on with invisible thread). A ribbon is tied over the wire to hide it. If you're worried about the sashes staying in place, pull the wire as tightly as you can to secure it. The panel on the top is just attached with hot glue, as is the ribbon trim. That's all there is to it. If you'd like to be more authentic, cut the sleeves of a poofy blouse and attach them to the spaghetti straps with hot-glue. Add big ribbons at the elbow, and you'll be almost authentic. To achieve the look of panniers (the puffs at the hips), stuff clothing or pillows under the skirt and secure them in place with wire tied under the waistband.

Dress III

This is the 20-minute costume solution. The shape of this dress said 1830, so it was transformed into a sleek gown for the Voodoo Queen, Marie Laveau. First, a generous coat of blood-red spray paint was applied to the entire dress, except for the belt, which was spray painted black. A black fringe was hot-glued near the bottom of the dress. Black tulle was stuffed into the sleeve openings and neckline to finish it off. Add a black headwrap and some large hoop earrings, and you'll enchant all who see you.

Basic Black & Other Witchwear

What would a witch (or warlock) wear? Your very own wardrobe may be the perfect place to start assembling a spooky or spectacular look for Halloween. Under ordinary circumstances, that black turtleneck you wear to work once a week may seem perfectly respectable, and even downright dull, but pair it with some black leggings, a pair of wings or spider legs, or a beak and it becomes the start of something sensational.

Before you go out and invest in costume materials, look deep into your own closet, keeping an eye out for simple shapes and lines, or interesting flourishes. Consider anything that you haven't worn in years a candidate for ripping, tearing, and cutting into a new costume-worthy shape. With a little imagination, a neglected and long-forgotten skirt becomes the basis of a mermaid tail (see page 26), and an old pair of pointy-toed shoes polish off a witch's ensemble. Your costume jewelry may seem too gaudy for everday, but it's perfect for Halloween when excess is the rule of the day.

A swim cap makes your hair disappear, leaving your head open for reinterpretation in any number of ways. Tights, when stretched over wire, can be fashioned into wings, and socks, when stuffed with cotton or fiberfill, look an awful lot like ears. Solid colored clothing of any kind in black, white, red, or green serves as the perfect backdrop for any costume that's witchy, devilish, mystical, or earthy. Remember the advice your mother gave you before heading out into the winter cold, and layer, layer, layer.

Simple Mask

Laundry list of costume basics:

Long or short black gloves
Tights in black, green, brown, white, or stripes
Scarves
Stretchy running pants or tops
Stretchy bicycle shorts
Long black or white skirt
Short black or white skirt
Black turtleneck, long-sleeved shirt or leotard
White turtleneck, long-sleeved shirt, or leotard
Capes of any kind
Swim caps or tight-fitting caps of any kind
Any clothing with interesting texture, such as faux fur
Crinoline or any other formalwear foundation garment
Old nightgown or slip
Old unfashionable boots (they're spraypaintable!)
Pointy shoes
Unfashionable, oversized men's suits
Costume jewelry
Old hats that can be painted, cut, or otherwise transformed

A basic premade black or white half-mask (available at craft stores) can be the base for any fantasy mask you can imagine. For a clean and elegant look, embellish a white mask with flowers—simply hot glue silk or other artificial

flowers to the edges or the entire surface. White sequin tape at the base of the flower petals on this mask makes for a more polished look. For more mystery, he hot-glued a veil to the bottom back edge of the mask. A premade mask base is also a perfect foundation for a leaf mask (see page 37) in the colors of summer or autumn. Leaves spray-painted gold or silver also make a dramatic impression. If you're going for a more sinister look, try a black premade mask base and add black or dark feathers.

Pumpkin Decorating

Pumpkin carving has been enjoyed for many, many years. A painted or decorated pumpkin can also be accented with carved sections. Some of the painting patterns provided also can be used as patterns for simple carvings!

The Basics

Before Beginning

The Gourd Family

Pumpkins are part of the gourd family, as are melons and squash. Pumpkins, melons and squash are considered to be fruit.

All gourds have thick, tough skins. Painting, carving, and embellishing can be done in the same manner on any variety.

Gourds are grown in several colors, including various shades of orange, yellow, green, brown, and white. Try picking a gourd in a color that will eventually be the background color for the chosen artwork. This will eliminate the need for a base coat.

Because of the unusual shapes of many gourds, a pumpkin turned on its side can utilize the stem as part of the design.

Because of the varying sizes of gourds (especially pumpkins!), the patterns provided can be adapted easily to fit any size. Once a determination has been made regarding the general size of the gourd to be used, an enlarged or a reduced photo copy of the pattern can be made.

Choosing the Perfect Pumpkin

When using a fresh pumpkin for painting, choose one that will suit the chosen pattern. When choosing one for carving, it is important that the complexity of the design be taken into consideration. Match more difficult designs to large, smooth, and/or flat pumpkins.

Always use fresh pumpkins that are free from bruises. Never purchase a pumpkin that does not have a stem. Once a stem has been broken off, the pumpkin will not last long. If a pumpkin can be chosen and picked from the vine, try to leave two to three inches of vine on the stem. This will allow the pumpkin to stay fresh longer.

Remember that once a pumpkin has been carved, its life expectancy is only two to five days.

Extending the Life of the Pumpkin

Pumpkins are considered seasonal fruit and, therefore, fresh ones cannot be found year round. Fresh pumpkins can be stored for several months under controlled conditions. They must always be kept dry and cool, and must not be allowed to freeze. When storing pumpkins, keep space around each pumpkin so that air can circulate. Never stack them—if one should get a rotten spot, it could infect the entire pile!

If the pumpkin dries out a little, it can be revived by soaking it in water for two to eight hours, then thoroughly drying.

In case fresh pumpkins cannot be found, the general instructions also include tips for painting on plastic pumpkins, compressed styrofoam pumpkins, papier-mâché pumpkins, and pumpkins made from wood.

Preparing Pumpkins for Carving

Cut an opening in the pumpkin using a large, sharp knife. Cut out the top for a lid or cut out the bottom. Cut the lid out at an angle. This provides a ledge for the lid to rest on. For easy alignment, cut a "key" in the lid so replacing the lid is simpler. It is recommended that lids on smaller pumpkins (less than 10" diameter) meas-

ure approximately 4" in diameter and lids on larger pumpkins (more than 10" diameter) measure approximately 6" to 8" in diameter.

Once an opening has been cut, clean out seeds and the inside membrane. Scrape out the inside lining of the pumpkin until the walls are approximately 1" thick.

Tools Needed for Pumpkin Carving

Few tools are needed for carving pumpkins, but they are important. A poking tool is used for transferring patterns, a pumpkin drill is used for making holes (such as eyes), and a saw tool is used for the actual carving. A large, sharp knife is needed to cut an opening in the pumpkin and a scraping tool makes cleaning out the pumpkin cavity easier.

Transfering Patterns onto Pumpkins

The pattern must first be adapted to a size that will work with the size of pumpkin being used. A photo copy, enlarged or reduced appropriately, is the easiest way to assure the design will be in proportion to the size of the pumpkin.

Transferring the pattern (see page 54) onto the chosen pumpkin can be done by first aligning the design in the proper position on the surface of the pumpkin. To allow the pattern to lie snugly on the round surface of the pumpkin, make cuts from the corners of the pattern toward the center and tape it into position.

The pattern can also be pinned to the pumpkin's surface, but to avoid unnecessary holes on the surface, it is recommended that the pins be placed in the center of the pattern or in the grooves on the pumpkin.

Once the pattern is in position, carefully punch holes along the outside of the pattern using a poking tool. Do not attempt to poke all the way through the pumpkin, just puncture the surface. For simpler designs, place the holes approximately 1/16" to 1/8" apart. If the designs are more intricate, holes are closer together. Once all the lines have been transferred, remove the pattern. If the "punched pattern" cannot easily be seen, dust the dots with flour.

Drilling Holes and Carving

- **Drilling Holes**

Before carving the design, drill holes as necessary for eyes and other small, round details using a pumpkin drill. Drilling requires applying pressure to the pumpkin; it must be done prior to carving. If not, the drilling process could break the design in areas that have been weakened by carving.

- **Carving**

To carve the design, use a saw tool to gently, but firmly, puncture the surface of the pumpkin. Once the saw tool has been inserted straight into the pumpkin, begin to saw from "dot to dot" at a 90° angle. Start carving from the center of the design and work outward. Do not twist or bend the saw tool; the blade could break.

The trick to perfect carving is patience. Once the carving is complete and all pieces are completely cut loose, use the eraser end of a pencil to gently push the carved pieces out. If a mistake should happen, try pinning the piece back in place using toothpicks or pins.

Candle Lighting the Carved Pumpkin

Rub vegetable oil or petroleum jelly onto freshly cut areas of the pumpkin to help delay aging. If possible, carve the pumpkin the day before it is to be displayed.

Cut a 1"-diameter hole in the top of the pumpkin over the candle to act as a chimney. This allows the air to circulate around the candle and will also prevent the candle from producing excess smoke. Pumpkins with smoke chimneys last longer because the heat can escape. Those that do not have chimneys will actually begin to bake from the inside out.

Place a candle inside, near the rear of the pumpkin on top of a piece of aluminum foil. When the candle is in position, carefully light it.

If no lid was cut out and the opening is in the bottom of the pumpkin, mount a candle on a cut piece of pumpkin, or place one in a household candle holder, or on a metal jar lid. Light the candle and then place the pumpkin over it.

If living in climates that get extremely cold (near freezing) at night or warmer than 60°F (15°C) in the day, bring the pumpkin inside to prolong its enjoyability!

Pumpkin Painting

The idea of painting on pumpkins is relatively new; it has allowed pumpkins to be used as a new art form.

Preparing Fresh Pumpkins for Painting

Because of the nature in which pumpkins are generally purchased, fresh pumpkins should be thoroughly washed and dried before patterns are transferred onto them.

Base Coating All Pumpkins

Sometimes a pumpkin will be painted with a design and the background will be left as the unpainted surface of the pumpkin. In some cases, the pattern requires that the entire pumpkin surface be painted. Acrylic paints have been used on the projects in this book and the number of coats necessary will be determined primarily by the base-coat color being used. If available, spray paint can also be used to base-coat pumpkins.

When fresh pumpkins are being used,a paint sealer should be used on the entire pumpkin surface before acrylic paint is applied. This will help adhere the paint to the surface. If a paint sealer is not used, paint can easily chip off. Because the surfaces of plastic, compressed styrofoam, papier mâché, and wooden pumpkins are rough and/or porous, a layer of paint sealer is not usually necessary.

Transfering Patterns onto Pumpkins

The pattern must first be adapted to a size that will work with the size of pumpkin being used. A photo copy, enlarged or reduced appropriately, is the easiest way to assure the design will be in proportion to the size of the chosen pumpkin. If all the colors in the pattern are dark, a color copy may be necessary to get the line definition needed for pattern transferring. To allow the pattern to lie snugly on the round surface of the pumpkin, make cuts from the corners of the pattern toward the center and tape it into position.

- **Method One**

The patterns in the book can be traced onto tracing paper and then transferred onto the pumpkin using graphite paper. Place the graphite paper between the pattern and the pumpkin with the graphite side facing the pumpkin. Tape the graphite paper and the pattern into position. Carefully, but firmly, trace the pattern using a pencil. Lift the corner slightly to make certain the pattern is transferring nicely. Once the design has been transferred, remove the pattern and the graphite paper.

• Method Two

Make a photo copy of the pattern in the appropriate size and cut it out. Place it on the pumpkin and tape into position. Carefully trace around the pattern. When using a fresh pumpkin, use a dull pencil or a blunt object and press hard enough to make a slight indentation on the pumpkin's surface, but be very careful not to puncture it. Once the design has been transferred, remove the pattern.

Paintbrushes & Sponges

Paintbrushes are the most common tools used for painting pumpkins. Good quality synthetic brushes work best when using acrylic paints. Sponges should be used when sponge painting and can be found in many different sizes and textures.

A variety of different sized paintbrushes are recommended—the size of the brush will depend upon the size of the pattern you are painting. Small, liner brushes are used for detailing and large, flat brushes are used for painting larger areas, such as base-coating. Flat chisel blenders, scrollers, and shaders might also come in handy, but are not mandatory.

Types of Brushes

Each brush has its own special purpose in painting. Drawing 1 shows the various types of brushes that are used in painting and detailing pumpkins.

Drawing 1

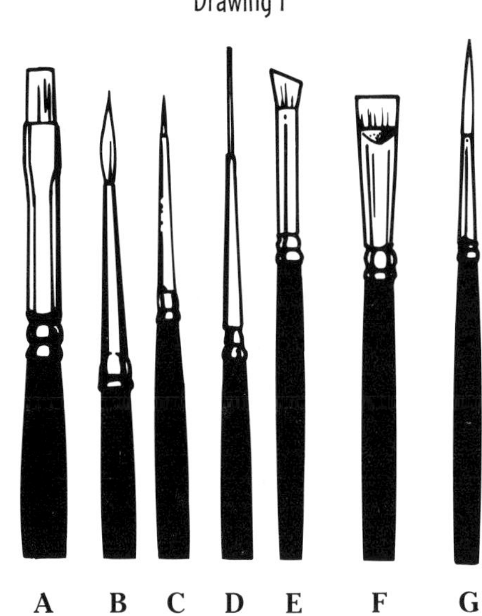

A-Flat brush
B-Round decorative
C-Short bristle round scroller brush
D-Script liner or scroller brush
E-Deerfoot brush
F-Fabric painting brush, flat scrubber brush
G-Fabric brush liner

• Brush Cleaning

Cleaner and conditioner can be used to thoroughly clean a brush before storage. It can also be used on hands and palettes. To clean the brushes when they have wet paint in them, work the cleaner into the bristles on a clean area of palette until the paint has loosened. Add small amounts of water as needed to create a lather. Rinse the brush thoroughly in cool water until no lather appears. If there is dried paint in the bristles, dip the brush in the cleaner and work the solution into the bristles on a clean area of the palette. Add small amounts of water to create a lather. Set the brush aside for 15 to 20 minutes. Repeat if necessary. Then rinse in cool water. When brushes have been thoroughly cleaned, store them with the bristle ends up.

Basic Tole Painting Techniques

• Solid Base Coating
Apply two to three coats of acrylic paint. This will give the best coverage and an even look to the paint.

• Base Coating Wash
When base-coating with a "wash," add water to the acrylic paint to achieve a sheer color. The amount of water used will determine the value of the color. Load brush with wash. Touch corner of brush on wet paper towel to remove excess water. When applying a wash, work as quickly as possible, using long, even strokes, but do not overlap.

• Sponge Painting
Load the top of a sponge with paint. Blot the sponge on a paper towel until most of the paint has been removed. Apply the paint to the pumpkin by lightly "blotting" the sponge up and down. Work in a circular motion starting at the center of the pumpkin.

• Highlighting and Shading
Dip a flat brush in water, then remove the excess water from the brush by blotting it on a paper towel. Apply acrylic paint to the side of the flat brush and blend, staying in one track, until the paint fades evenly across the brush. The paint will fade from dark to light.

• Stippling
Load a dry round fabric brush or stipple brush with paint. Use very little paint. Bounce brush on paper towel to remove excess paint, then apply lightly. Vary dot sizes to create shadow or texture effect.

• Dots
Use a round object such as the end of a paintbrush, stylus, or corsage pin. Dip in paint, then on project. For uniform dots, load brush each time a dot is made. For descending dots, load the brush then start "dotting" until they get smaller and smaller. Create small dots by using a liner brush and rolling it to a point. For hearts, create two dots side by side, and then drag the brush or stylus through the dots making the point of the heart.

• Spattering
To apply speckles to the surface, select an old toothbrush or similar stiff bristled brush. Thin the paint with water, load the brush and rub the bristles across the edge of a palette knife. The thinner the paint the larger the dots or speckles.

• Comma Strokes
Use a round brush to create a dot. Rotate and decrease pressure as the tail of the comma or tear is created.

• Slip Slapping
Load a flat brush with paint using a swift criss-cross motion.

• Dry Brushing
Dip a flat brush in a small amount of acrylic paint. Remove the excess paint from the brush by working in a criss-cross motion on a paper towel. Using the same motion, lightly apply the paint to the pumpkin.

• Outlining
Painters with a great deal of detail painting experience most generally opt to detail paint using a liner brush. Painters with little or no experience will want to use a fine or medium-point permanent marker.

When using a liner brush, load in paint thinned with water. Pull the brush through the paint, turning to get a fine point. Hold the brush perpendicular to the work and line the desired areas. The thickness of the line will be determined by the amount of pressure applied to the brush.

• **Detail Painting**

The experience of the painter usually determines how the pumpkin will be detailed and outlined.

Crackle Medium

Apply a base coat of one to two coats using either purple or dark blue. When dry, apply an even coat of crackle medium and allow to dry thoroughly. Apply a coat of the contrasting color vermillion and yellow light 1:1. Do NOT apply paint too thickly. It will have more crackle if the paint is thinner.

Varnishing

Apply varnish with a clean, soft brush, using a slip-slap motion and a medium application. The first coat may have a tendency to pull apart and act as though it does not want to stick. Work it with the brush and the slip-slap motion until it adheres and starts to dry. Reload brush and move onto another area until the entire piece is covered. Let dry and recoat three times. This finish, after reaching cure (two weeks), is alcohol resistant.

Sealing the Artwork

After the artwork is complete and the paint is completely dry, it is recommended that an acrylic spray sealer be used to set the paint and protect the artwork. Either matte sealer or gloss sealer can be used depending on the look that is desired.

Pumpkin Embellishing

Pumpkin embellishing adds interest to any painted or carved pumpkin. In many cases, embellishing is the final, finishing touch that brings the creation to life. Embellishments can also be used on pumpkins that have not been painted or carved!

Adhesives for Embellishing

Many types of adhesives can be used to adhere embellishments to real or hand made pumpkins: hot glue gun and glue sticks, craft glue, and industrial-strength glue.

Hot glue is the most common adhesive used in this book; however, it can be substituted with other types of adhesive. If a pumpkin is going to be displayed outdoors where the temperature is cold, hot glue is not recommended and should be substituted with industrial-strength glue. However, if a pumpkin is going to be displayed indoors, hot glue is a good choice.

Plastic pumpkins are manufactured from different types of plastic and in varying thicknesses. Because of this, it is recommended that hot glue not be used on plastic pumpkins. The plastic could possibly melt from the heat of the glue.

If a pumpkin has been sprayed with a product that does not allow adhesives to adhere properly, straight pins can be used to secure embellishments in place.

Materials Used for Hair

Most pumpkins are painted or carved with a "face" and therefore lend themselves to hair styles that add personality and character.

Make hair from actual wigs and wiglets, doll hair, curly yarn, fake fur, crinkled paper-grass, fabric strips, curling ribbon, straw, wire, and polyester stuffing and feathers. All of these choices are available in several different colors. Polyester stuffing can be spray-painted with any color!

Using Craft Foam Sheets

Craft foam is available in many different colors and is a great medium for embellishing. It can be cut into any shape and easily glued to pumpkins. If the craft foam shapes are not as secure as needed, straight pins can be used to help secure the pieces in place. Craft foam can be highlighted with acrylic paints.

Making Ears and Antennae

Make antennae easily using wire or pipe cleaners and styrofoam balls or beads.

The easiest way to make ears is to cut felt fabric into triangles and simply hot-glue them into place on top of the pumpkin.

Ears can also be made by using wire bent into any shape and size. The wire can be left uncovered or can be covered with any type of fabric by cutting the fabric to size and gluing it to the fronts and backs of the shaped wire ears. Poke the wire ends into the top of the pumpkin and shape as desired.

Fabric Stiffener

All-purpose sealer is used to stiffen and give added body to fabric. Cut the desired shape out of fabric larger than the final size. Lay down freezer paper with the shiny side up. Thin the all-purpose sealer with either water or flow medium 2:1. Using a soft bristle brush, apply a thick coat that saturates the back of the fabric. Allow to dry completely. Peel off of the freezer paper and cut to the desired size. Fabric should have an even sheen on the BACK side. Clean up with soap and cool water.

Bats and Ghosts

Materials:

Doll hair: white curly
Fabric paint: black
Floral wire: 12" lengths, black, white (4 each)
Foam sheet: black
Glue gun and glue sticks
Rhinestones: multi-colored, small
Styrofoam balls: 1" (3), 2" (1)

Carving:

Carve pumpkin, referring to pattern and General Instructions.

Decorating:

Cut two large and four small bats from foam. Hot-glue large bats to front of pumpkin. Attach small bats to black wires. Twist and bend wires. Insert into top of pumpkin. To make ghosts, cut styrofoam balls in half. Cover round portion of balls with doll hair, allowing hair to dangle. Hot-glue large ghosts and one small ghost to pumpkin as desired. Attach remaining small ghosts to white wires. Twist and bend wires. Insert into top of pumpkin. Hot-glue rhinestones to large bat wings as desired. Hot-glue rhinestones to bats and ghosts for eyes and mouths. Paint dots around carved openings with fabric paint.

Turkey

Materials:

Acrylic paints: black, dk. brown, lt. brown, orange, red, white, yellow
Feathers: assorted colors
Foam mount board: 5" x 8"
Craft knife
Masking tape
Sandpaper: 80 grit
Straight pins
Tape: masking

Painting:

Enlarge turkey head pattern to fit pumpkin. Cut turkey head from mount board with exacto knife. Sand edges of head. Paint and detail head, referring to pattern.

Decorating:

Arrange feathers and attach to back of pumpkin with straight pins and secure with masking tape. Attach head to front of pumpkin with straight pins.

Bountiful Harvest

Materials:

Straw hat
Pumpkin: 6" wood, prepainted
Vegetables and/or fruit pick
Glue gun and glue sticks
Leaves: silk autumn

Decorating:

Hot-glue crown of hat to pumpkin. Clip small clusters of leaves from stem. Glue leaves along bottom of pumpkin and back in crown, behind pumpkin. Separate portions of floral pick and glue along bottom of pumpkin. Fill in with more leaves, if needed.

Button Punkin'

Materials:

Fabric: orange wool, 1/3 yd
Buttons, old: dk. colored (12 for mouth), round gold (1 for nose), large round lt. colored (2 for eyes)
Dried leaves and vines
Floss: ivory cotton perle (1 ball)
Glue gun and glue sticks.
Needle
Sewing machine
Stem: 1½"-diameter x 6"
Straight pins
Stuffing
Thread: coordinating

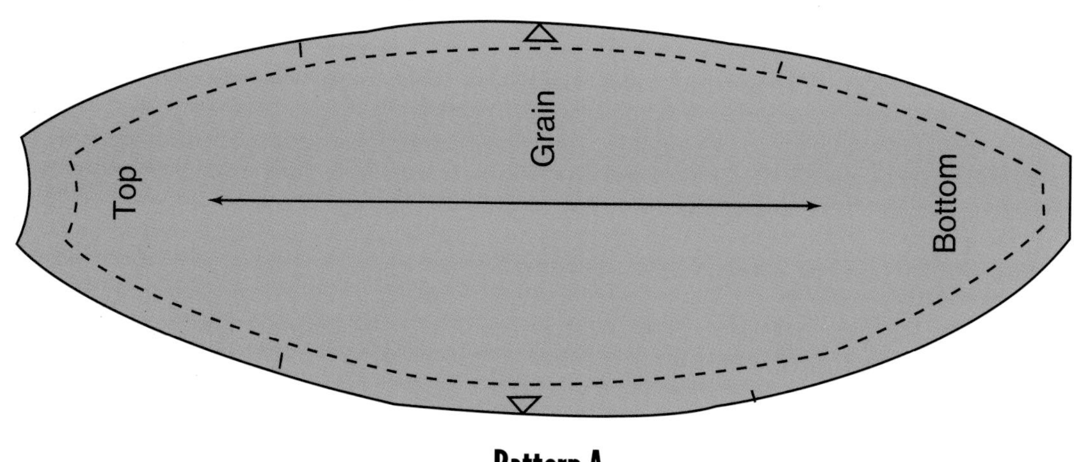

Pattern A

Decorating:

Enlarge Pattern A 200%. Cut six of Pattern A from wool fabric, transferring all markings. Pin two panels right sides together, matching notches. Sew a 1/4" seam along one side of panel. With right sides together, pin and sew a third panel to first two panels. Set aside. Repeat process with remaining three panels. With right sides together, pin and sew panel sets together, beginning and ending 1 1/2" from top. Clip curves and turn right side out. Stuff firmly. Turn top edge in 1/2". Whip-stitch 1 1/2" seams closed. Place stem into opening and hot-glue in place. Cut floss into two 12" lengths. Thread through each eye button and tie into a bow. Hot-glue eyes to pumpkin, referring to photograph for placement. Cut floss into twelve 8" lengths. Cut each length in half. Double-thread through each mouth button and tie into a knot. Hot-glue mouth buttons to pumpkin. Hot-glue round gold nose button to pumpkin. Hot-glue dried leaves and vines around base of stem.

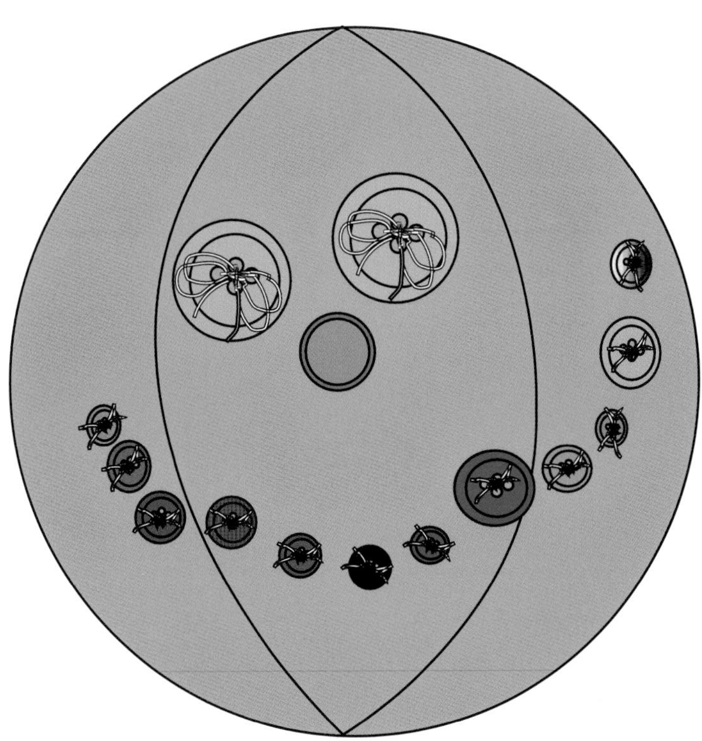

Straw Hat

Materials:

Acrylic paints: aqua, black, dk. green, dusty pink, red, dk. red, white
Glue gun and glue sticks
Leaf stem: silk with two leaves
Ribbon: 2"-wide black-and-white polka-dot, 1 1/2 yds
Straw hat: orange
Tree branch: 2"

Painting:

Referring to pattern and General Instructions, paint and detail top of hat as follows: **base**–eyes white; irises dk. green; pupils black; nose and mouth red; **float** (shade)–eyes aqua; nose dk. red; **float** (highlight)–pupils aqua; nose and mouth dusty pink; **stipple**–cheeks dusty pink; **line**–eyebrows, eyelashes, eyes, nose and mouth black; **comma strokes**–eyes, nose and mouth white; **dots**–eyes, nose and mouth white.

Decorating:

Roll up edges of hat brim to form a triangle. Secure with hot glue. Hot-glue leaf stem to top of hat, referring to photograph for placement. Tie ribbon into bow at base of brim for a bow tie.

Birdhouse

Materials:

Gourd: papier mâché
Acrylic paints: black, green, orange, dk. orange, white
Glue gun and glue sticks
Craft knife
Leaf stem (perch)
Raffia: natural, 1 yd

Carving:

Cut one 2"-diameter circle in gourd, referring to photograph for placement.

Painting:

Referring to pattern and General Instructions, paint and detail gourd as follows: **base**–entire gourd orange; **lettering**–black; **wash**–border and door strips white; check pattern green; **float** (shade)–border strips dk. orange; **spatter**–front of gourd dk. orange.

Decorating:

Hot-glue leaf stem to inside of opening for perch, referring to photograph for placement. Tie raffia into a double-loop bow around stem of gourd. Knot ends. Gently spread raffia open.

B-O-O!

Materials:

Pumpkins: papier mâché, small (3)
Acrylic paints: black, bright blue, dk. orange, lt. orange
Leaves: silk (4)
Pencil
Raffia: natural, 2 yds
Straight pins
Wire: light-weight green 2 yds
Wire cutters

Painting:

Referring to pattern and General Instructions, paint and detail pumpkins as follows: **base**–entire pumpkin dk. orange; **Dry-brush**–with lt. orange: **Detail**–lettering black; **line**–bright blue.

Decorating:

Cut raffia into three equal lengths. Knot ends. Tie into bows around stems of pumpkins. Secure bow to stems with straight pins. Cut wire into three equal lengths. Wrap wires around pencil to form vines. Wrap a wire vine around each pumpkin stem. Attach a leaf or two to base of each pumpkin stem. Secure with straight pins.

Clown

Materials:

Acrylic paints: black, lt. blue, bright orange, pink, white
Clown's hat
Craft glue
Novelty item: clown nose
Straight pins

Painting:

Paint and detail pumpkin, referring to pattern.

Decorating:

Glue nose to pumpkin face. Attach hat to pumpkin with straight pins.

Silhouette Pumpkin

Materials:

Acrylic paint: black
Candle: 2 1/2" diameter

Painting:

Paint and detail pumpkin, referring to pattern.

Carving:

Carve hole 1/2" deep into top of pumpkin same diameter as candle. Insert candle.

Dressed to Fill

Materials:

Bucket: 7 qt. yellow
Acrylic paints: black, gray, dk. green, lt. green, dusty pink, lt. purple, red, dk. red, white
Fabric: black candy corn print, 1/4 yd
Glue gun and glue sticks
Needle: hand-sewing
Sealer: all-purpose
Thread: black
Tissue paper: (1 sheet)

Painting:

Mix each paint color with all-purpose sealer 2:1 for best adhesion. Referring to pattern and General Instructions, paint and detail tub as follows: **base**–eyes and tooth white; irises dk. green; pupils black; cheeks and nose red; **float** (shade)–eyes and tooth lt. purple; cheeks and nose dk. red; **float** (highlight)–irises lt. green; pupils gray; cheeks and nose dusty pink; **line**–eyebrows, eyelashes, eyes, cheeks, nose, mouth and tooth black; **comma strokes**–eyes, nose and cheeks white; **dots**–eyes, cheeks and nose white.

Decorating:

Cut fabric into one 7" x 11" piece and one 4" x 4 1/2" piece. With right sides together, fold larger piece of fabric in half lengthwise. Sew from each end around to the center, leaving a 2" opening in the center. Turn right side out. Tear tissue paper in half and stuff each end of fabric. Sew opening closed. Equally fold 4 1/2" sides of smaller fabric to center. Wrap and pull around center of larger fabric to form a bow tie. Hot-glue ends together. Hot-glue bow tie to bottom of bucket. Fill as desired.

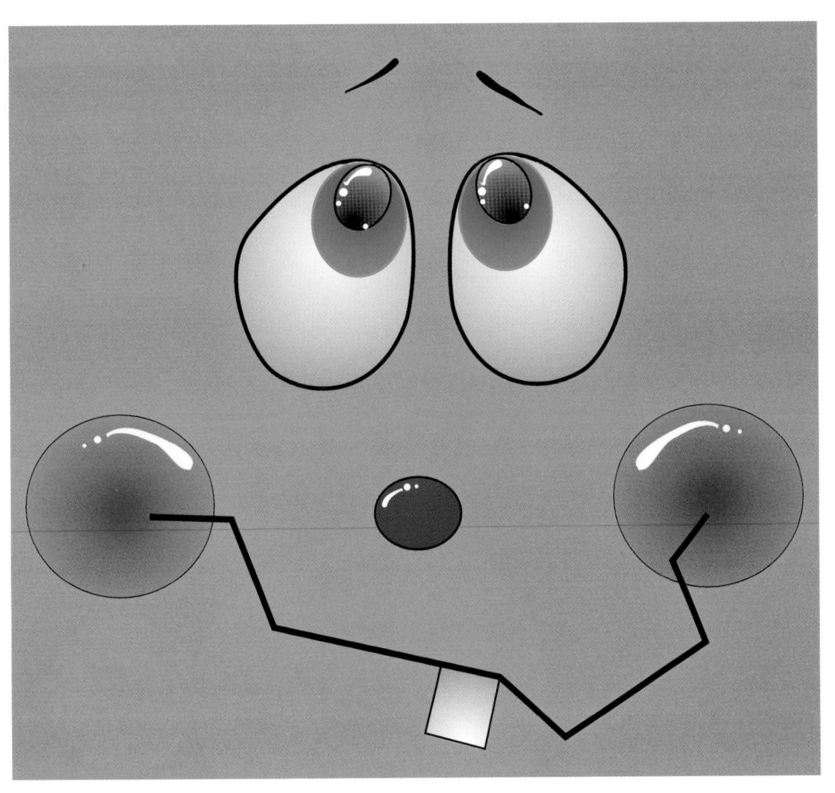

Snider the Spider

Materials:

Pumpkin: compressed styrofoam
Acrylic paints: aqua, black, dk. gray, lt. gray, green, dk. green, magenta, peach, purple, lt. purple, red, dk. red, white
Balls: wooden, 2" (body), 1" (head)
Chenille: 12" lengths, white (4)
Crackle medium
Craft glue
Glue gun and glue sticks
Ribbon: 1"-wide iridescent burgundy/gray ombré wire-edge, 3/8 yd

Painting:

Paint pumpkin as in "Toadal" Spell. See page 98. Lightly **dry-brush** chenille legs with black. Hot-glue head to body and **base-coat** with black. Referring to pattern and General Instructions, paint and detail spider as follows: **base**–eyes white; irises green; pupils black; nose and mouth red; spots lt. purple; **float** (shade)–eyes aqua; irises dk. green; nose and mouth dk. red; medium and large spots purple; **float** (highlight)–nose and mouth peach; medium and large spots magenta; **line**–eyebrows, eyelashes and eyes dk. gray; **additional detail lining**–eyebrows and eyelashes lt. gray; **comma strokes**–eyes white; hearts on mouth peach; **dots**–eyes white.

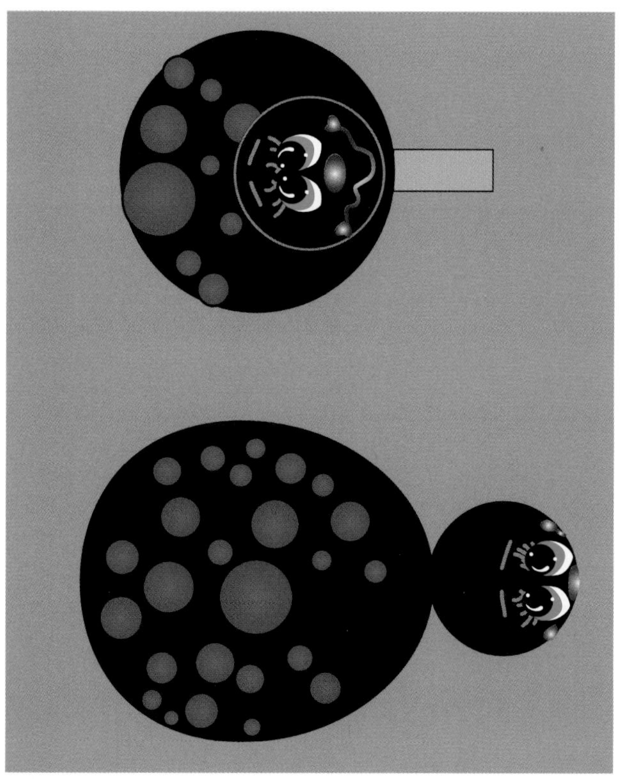

Decorating:

Center and hot-glue legs under body. Bend chenille ends for feet. Tie ribbon into bow. Hot-glue bow in place. Tack feet to pumpkin where desired.

Bagged Pumpkin

Materials:

Fabric: muslin, 1/2 yd
Acrylic paints: black, dk. green, bright red, white
Jute: 1 yd
Lace: 3/4"-wide, 3/4 yd
Stuffing. Sewing machine
Straight pins
Tea Bags: (2)
Textile medium
Thread: coordinating

Decorating:

Cut muslin fabric into two 11" x 15 1/2" pieces. With right sides together, sew a 1/4" seam along sides and bottom of rectangle to form a bag. Turn right side out. Fold top edges in 1/4" and press. Pin and sew lace around top edges. Place tea bags into a pot of boiling water and allow to steep for a few minutes. Immerse bag in pot until desired color is achieved. Remove bag from pot and lay flat to dry. Transfer pattern onto bag and paint as instructed in Painting below. Fill bag with stuffing. Tie jute around corners. Hand-gather
top of bag. Wrap jute around bag, gather and tie into bow.

Painting:

Mix each paint color with textile medium 1:1. **Dry-brush** and detail bag, referring to pattern.

Hearts

Materials:

Acrylic paints: black, mauve, smoked pearl, dk. red, white
Glue gun and glue sticks
Rhinestones
Ribbon: 2"-wide pastel rainbow wire-edge ombré, 1 yd
Wooden hearts: large (2), small (1), miniature (2)

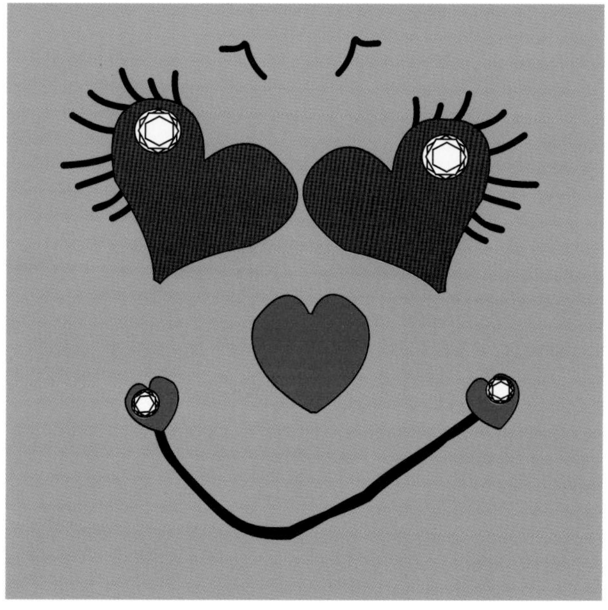

Painting:

Referring to pattern and General Instructions, paint and detail pumpkin as follows: **base**–large hearts black; small and miniature hearts dk. red; **float** (highlight)–large hearts smoked pearl; small and miniature hearts mauve; **line**–eyebrows, eyelashes and mouth black (after hearts are attached to pumpkin).

Decorating:

Hot-glue rhinestones to large and miniature hearts, referring to pattern for placement. Hot-glue hearts to pumpkin. Tie ribbon into bow around stem of pumpkin.

BOO

Materials:

Fabric paint: black
Glue gun and glue sticks
Novelty items: cats, pumpkins, black streamers, white streamers
Ribbon: 1/2"-wide black candy corn print, 1 yd; 1"-wide green/orange check with pumpkin print, 1 yd

Carving:

Carve pumpkin, referring to pattern and General Instructions.

Painting:

Outline carving with a dot pattern using fabric paint.

Decorating:

Tie ribbons into bows. Hot-glue bows to top of pumpkin. Drape ribbon tails. Arrange and insert novelty items as desired.

Frank

Materials:

Acrylic paints: black, bright green, dk. green, red, yellow
Bolts: large (2)
Glue gun and glue sticks
Novelty items: blood, hair, black, teeth
Straight pins
Wire: 12"
Wire cutters

Painting:

Paint pumpkin dk. green. Lightly sponge bright green over dk. green. Paint and detail pumpkin face, referring to pattern. **Dry-brush** dark circles under eyes and enhance chin with black.

Decorating:

Cut a small portion of hair to form two thick, rectangular eyebrows. Hot-glue in place on pumpkin. Style and hot-glue hair to pumpkin, leaving a high brow. Attach teeth with pins. Paint lips to blend with pumpkin face. Cut wire into small lengths and insert into forehead for stitches. Screw bolts into side of pumpkin. Dab blood around stitches and bolts.

Pirate

Materials:

Acrylic paints: black, white
Bandana
Felt: 8" x 10" black
Glue gun and glue sticks
Straight pins
Witch's wig

Painting:

Remove stem from pumpkin. Paint and detail pumpkin, referring to pattern.

Decorating:

Cut eye patch and patch straps from felt. Paint skull and cross-bones on eye patch. Hot-glue over left eye. Attach wig to pumpkin with straight pins. Attach bandana to pumpkin with straight pins.

Trick or Treat Bucket

Materials:

Bucket: 7"-diameter, metal

Acrylic paints: black, purple, bright red, dk. red, white, lt. yellow, dk. yellow

Ribbon: 1½"-wide wire-edge purple, 1¼ yds; purple-check, 1¼ yds

Texture paste

Painting:

Mix bright red and lt. Yellow 1:1 for basecoat. Mix basecoat with texture paste 1:1 and paint outside of bucket. Let dry thoroughly. Paint lip of bucket purple. Paint face on bucket, referring to pattern. Let dry thoroughly.

Decorating:

Tightly wrap purple ribbon around handle of bucket. Cut purple-check ribbon into two equal lengths. Referring to photograph, tie each ribbon into a bow around end of handle.

Witch

Materials:

Acrylic paints: bright green, dk. green, red, yellow
Fabric paint: black
Glue gun and glue sticks
Novelty items: latex skin; teeth; wig, black
Sponge
Straight pins
Witch's hat

Painting:

Form latex skin into a long nose and several warts. Press in place on pumpkin. Paint nose, warts and pumpkin dk. green. Paint and detail pumpkin face, referring to pattern. **Sponge** face with bright green.

Decorating:

Hot-glue wig to top of pumpkin. Cut a small portion of hair from wig and hot-glue for eyebrows and to stick out of warts. Attach teeth with straight pins. Paint lips to blend with pumpkin face. Shape hat as desired with straight pins to pumpkin.

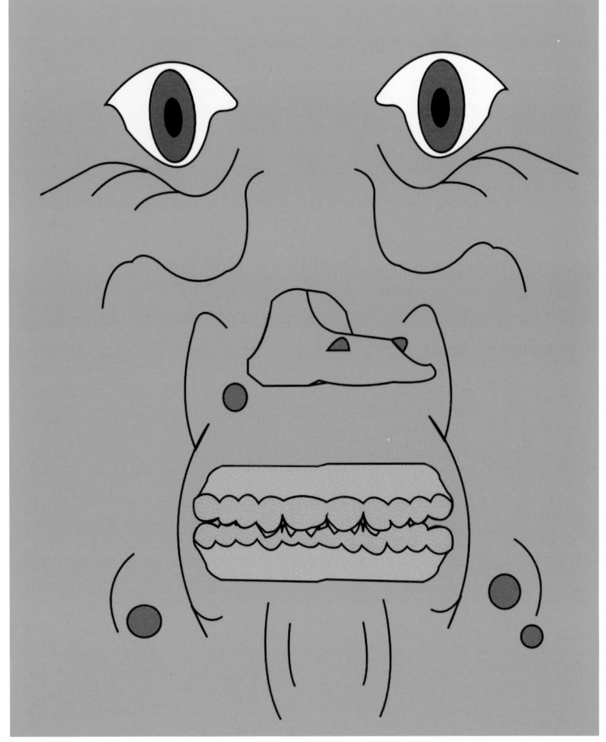

Scarecrow

Materials:

Buttons: 1" blue (2)
Foam sheets: orange, red, yellow
Newspaper
Permanent marker: black
Raffia: natural: Rope, 1 1/2 yds
Rubber bands
Straight pins
Straw hat
Styrofoam ball: 2"
Toddler clothes: overalls and shirt
Twist ties

Decorating:

Cut styrofoam ball in half for eyes. Hot-glue buttons to eyes for pupils. Hot-glue eyes to pumpkin. Cut a triangle from red foam sheet for nose and hot-glue in place. Cut mouth from yellow foam sheet. Hot-glue mouth to pumpkin. Cut two circles from orange foam sheet for cheeks and hot-glue in place. Outline nose, mouth and cheeks with stitch marks using black marker. Cut an 18" length of raffia. Tie raffia in center with twist ties. Hot-glue raffia on top of pumpkin for hair. Attach straw hat to top of pumpkin with pins. Button shirt and loosely stuff with newspaper. Pull overalls over shirt and stuff until body is firm. Cut four 6" lengths of raffia. Fold raffia lengths in half and secure folds with rubber bands. Insert a raffia bundle into arms and legs. Cut rope into four 5" lengths. Tie and knot rope around shirt and pant cuffs to hold raffia in place. Tie remaining rope around waist for belt. Attach body to pumpkin with pins.

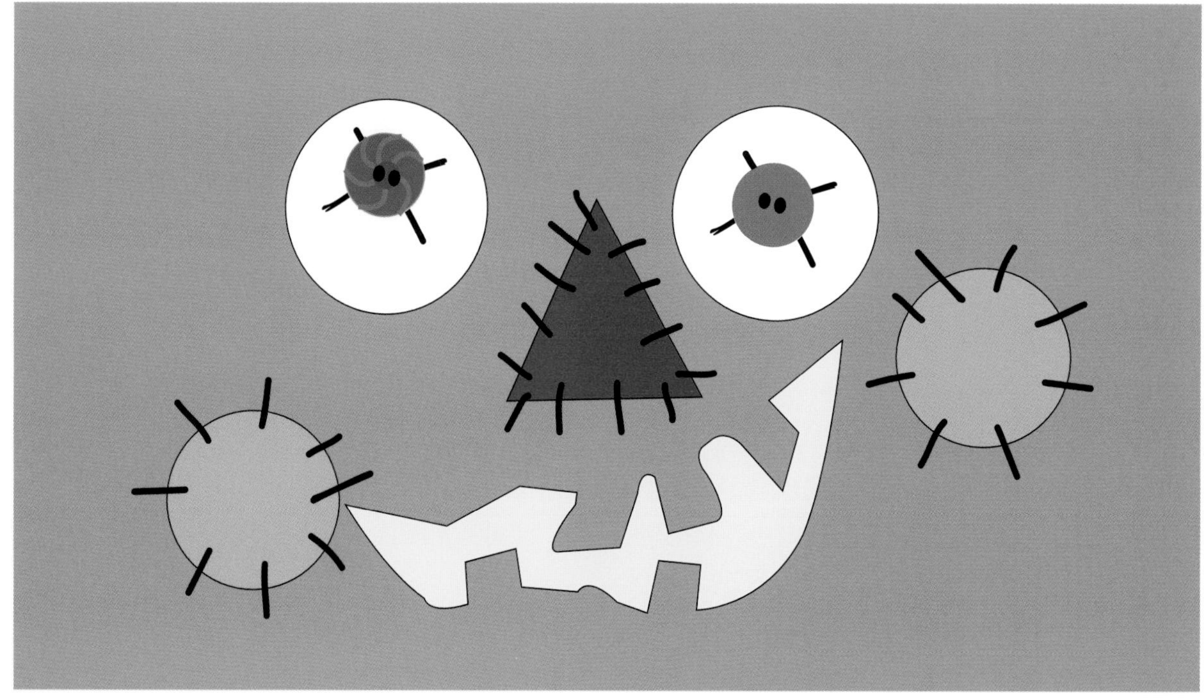

Bert & Ernie

Materials:

Acrylic paints: black, white
Feathers: black
Foam sheets: green, red
Glue gun and glue sticks
Styrofoam balls: 2" (2)

Carving:

Refer to patterns and General Instructions.

Decorating:

Cut two 2"-diameter circles from green foam sheet and two from red foam sheet. Cut styrofoam balls in half for eyes. Paint a black circle in center of each eye. Add a dot of white paint to each black circle. Referring to photograph for placement, hot-glue a pair of eyes to green foam circles and a pair to red foam circles, slightly off center. Hot-glue eyes to pumpkins. Hot-glue feathers above eyes for eyebrows and around stems for hair.

Girlfriend

Materials:

Acrylic paints: black, dusty blue, mauve,
lt. purple, red, dk. red, white
Button: 1" gold
Doily: 5" square
Battenburg, white
Glue gun and glue sticks
Novelty item: eyelashes
Ribbon: 1/2"-wide gold metallic mesh, 1 yd

Painting:

Referring to pattern and General Instructions, paint and detail pumpkin as follows: **base**–eyes white; irises dusty blue; pupils and mole black; nose and mouth red; **float** (shade)–eyes lt. purple; nose and mouth dk. red; **float** (highlight)–nose and mouth mauve; additional highlights in mouth white; **stipple**–cheeks red; **line**–eyebrows and eyes black; nose and mouth dk. red; **comma strokes**–eyes white; **dots**–eyes white.

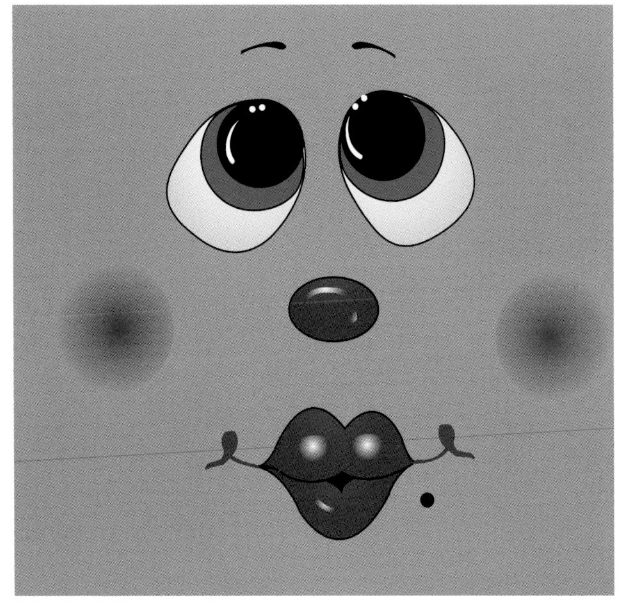

Decorating:

Cut doily in half. Hot-glue to bottom of pumpkin for collar. Hot-glue button to center of collar for a brooch. Hot-glue eyelashes to top of eyes. Wrap ribbon around pumpkin for head band and tie into bow at top. Tuck ribbon tails under band.

Robot

Materials:

Buttons: 1" sun-shaped (2)
Dryer venting: flexible aluminum, 2 1/2 yds
Facial tissue box: boutique-size
Foam sheets: green, red, white
Glue gun and glue sticks
Knife: serrated
Pen: black felt marker
Reflective ribbon tape: 1 1/2 yds
Rhinestones: large, round red and yellow
Spray paint: silver
Straight pins
Styrofoam ball: 1 1/2"
Wire: bailing, 1 yd
Wire cutters

Decorating:

Spray paint tissue box and pumpkin. Let dry thoroughly. Place open end of tissue box over stem and hot-glue onto pumpkin for head. Attach reflective ribbon tape around top of tissue box. Cut styrofoam ball in half for eyes. Hot-glue eyes on head, referring to photograph for placement. Hot-glue buttons onto eyes for pupils. Coil wire and hot-glue ends to sides of head for antenna. Draw a rectangle with black felt marker for mouth. Cut two narrow rectangles from green foam sheet for lips and hot-glue in place. Cut dryer venting into four equal lengths with serrated knife. Hot-glue and pin venting pieces to pumpkin for arms and legs. Attach reflective ribbon tape around ends of each venting piece. Cut green foam sheet into one 6" square. Draw lines for control panel with black felt marker. Cut one 2" square from red foam sheet and white foam sheet and hot-glue to control panel. Hot-glue rhinestones to control panel.

Cowboy

Materials:

Acrylic paints: black, brown, red, white
Bandanna
Glue gun and glue sticks
Straw hat

Painting:

Referring to pattern and General Instructions, paint and detail pumpkin as follows: **base**–eyes white; irises brown; pupils black; cheeks and nose red; **line**–eyes, mouth and stitches black; **dots**–eyes white.

Decorating:

Hot-glue hat to pumpkin. Tie bandanna around base of pumpkin, referring to photograph. Secure to pumpkin with hot glue.

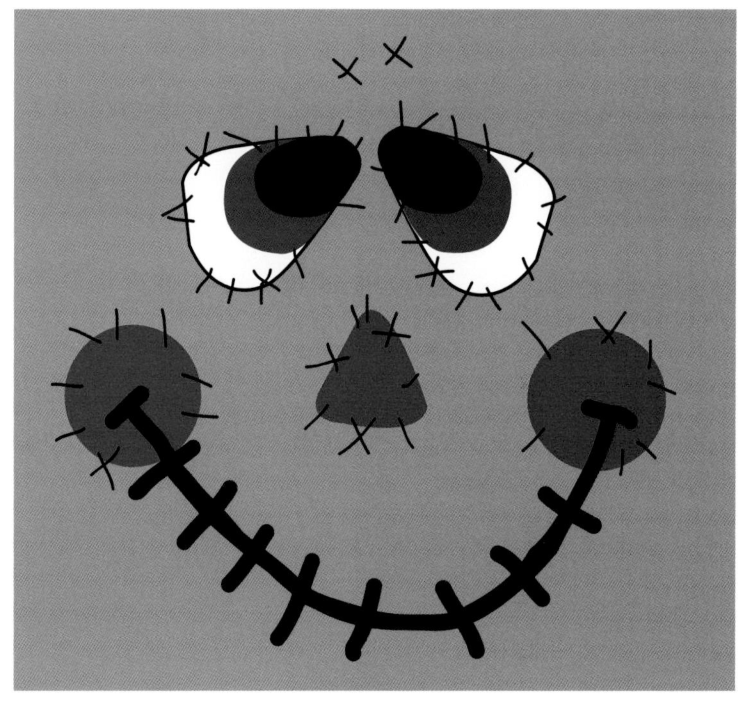

Vampire

Materials:

Acrylic paints: black, black-green, red, white
Black felt squares (5)
Glue gun and glue sticks
Stapler and staples

Painting:

Paint and detail pumpkin, referring to pattern.

Decorating:

Sew two felt squares right sides together to create a vampire's collar. Sew a large dart along seam. Fold open and sew along edges of dart to form back collar. Cut felt square into one 7"x 9" piece and one 2" x 4" piece. Pleat large piece like a bow tie. Fold small piece in half lengthwise and wrap around center of bow tie. Staple in back. Staple two corners of remaining two felt squares together for front collar. Center stapled corners at bottom front of pumpkin. Wrap collar around sides of pumpkin, stapling to secure. Center back collar at back of pumpkin and wrap collar around sides, stapling to secure. Hot-glue bow tie to front of pumpkin.

A Ghostly Face

Materials:

Acrylic paints: black, brown, gray, dk. gray, dk. green, dusty pink, dk. red, white
Glue gun and glue sticks
Novelty eyes: small (4)
Varnish: gloss
Watercolor paper: 11" x 16", 400 lb. cold-pressed, white

Painting:

Cut ghost from watercolor paper. Referring to pattern and General Instructions, paint and detail ghost on smooth side of paper as follows: **base**–eyes white; irises dk. green; pupils black; **float** (shade)–eyes, mouth and outer edge of ghost gray; **float** (highlight)–outer edge of ghost

dusty pink; **stipple**–cheeks dusty pink; **line**–eyebrows, eye lashes, eyes and mouth black; **comma stroke**–eyes white; **dots**–eyes white; **spatter**–entire ghost dk. gray. Apply a coat of varnish to both sides of paper. Bend and shape paper while still damp. Let dry thoroughly. Apply a second coat of varnish and further bend and shape paper as desired.

Paint and detail pumpkin as follows:

Base–eyes white; irises brown; pupils and cracks black; mouth and nose dk. red; **float** (shade)–nose dusty pink; **stipple**–cheeks dusty pink; **line**–eyelashes, eyes, nose and mouth black; **dots**–eyes and nose white.

Decorating:

Hot-glue ghost and pairs of novelty eyes to pumpkin, referring to photograph and diagram for placement.

Jack Frost

Materials:

Pumpkins: compressed styrofoam (3- small, medium, large)
Acrylic paints: black, antique med. brown, red, white, yellow
Clothing: winter cap and a pair of mittens
Fabric: 54"-wide wool plaid, 1/4 yd
Glue gun and glue sticks
Craft knife
Pen: medium pt. permanent black marker
Spray sealer: pearl finish
Stuffing
Twigs: 18" (2), 12" (1)
Twine. Wood: 1/4" thick balsa, 5" x 9"

Painting:

Cut sign from balsa wood with craft knife. Paint sign with antique med. brown. Paint lettering with black. Paint and detail pumpkins, referring to pattern and photo for placement. Outline eyes, mouth, and candy corns with black marker.

Decorating:

Referring to photograph, stack and hot-glue pumpkins together. Push 18" twigs into middle pumpkin for arms. Loosely stuff mittens and tie onto ends of arms with twine. Hot-glue hat onto pumpkin head. Wrap wool fabric around neck for scarf. Hot-glue 12" twig to back of sign. Hot-glue sign to palm of left mitten.

Werewolf

Materials:

Acrylic paints: brown, flesh, ivory, yellow
Glue gun and glue sticks
Novelty items: fangs; hair, brown and white; latex skin
Sponge
Straight pins

Painting:

Form latex skin into nose. Press in place on pumpkin. Paint nose brown with flesh nostrils. Paint pumpkin flesh. Paint and detail pumpkin face, referring to pattern. **Sponge** face with brown.

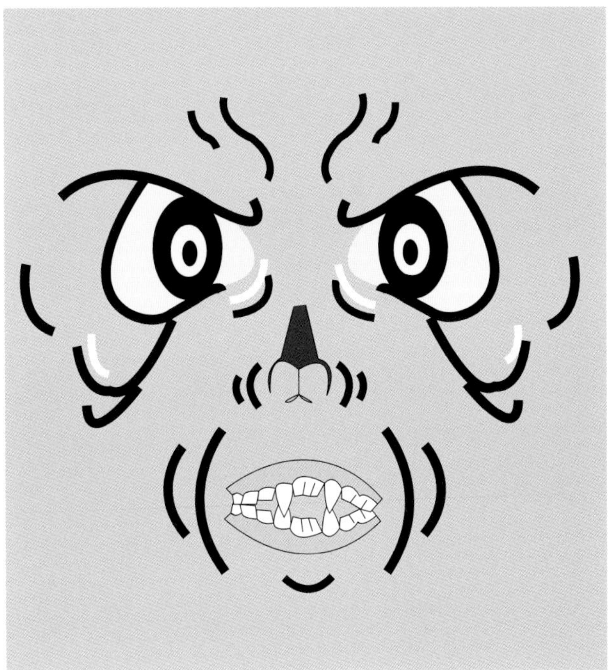

Decorating:

Hot-glue brown hair to pumpkin, referring to photograph for placement. Add white hair to form stripes. Attach fangs with pins.

Grim Reaper

Materials:

Acrylic paints: white, yellow
Crepe: black, 1/2 yd
Glue gun and glue sticks
Nails: (2)
Novelty items: skeleton hand, hatchet
Spray paint: black

Painting:

Spray pumpkin black. Paint and detail pumpkin face, referring to pattern.

Decorating:

Wrap and shape black crepe around face of pumpkin to form a hood. Hot-glue skeleton hand to side of face so it appears to be pulling hood back. Attach hatchet to back of pumpkin with nails.

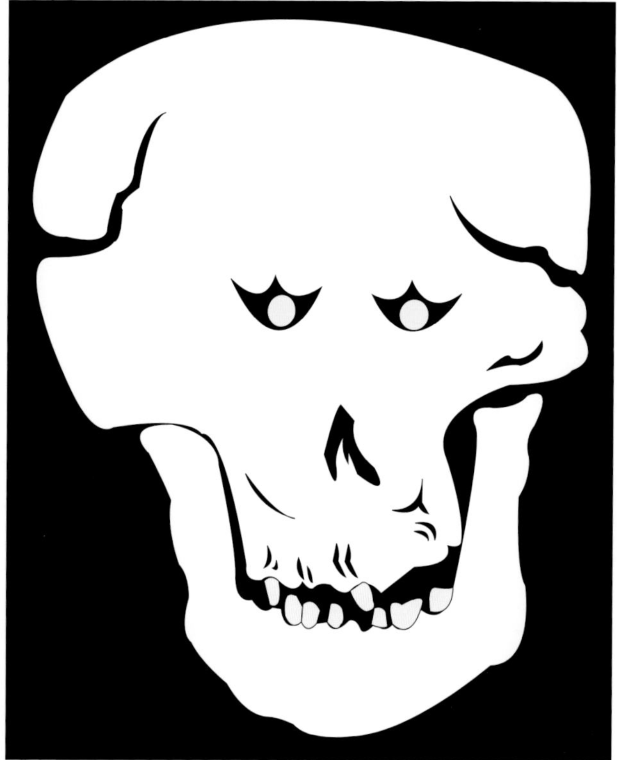

Welcome

Materials:

Pumpkin: large compressed styrofoam
Acrylic paints: aqua, black, green, bright green, magenta, lt. purple, lt. yellow
Glaze: glitter
Glue gun and glue sticks
Pencil
Ribbon: 1 1/2"-wide pastel plaid 1 1/2 yds
Stars: wooden with two holes—large (1), medium (3), small (3); miniature, no holes (2)
Varnish: clear
Wire: 16 gauge, 4 ft
Wire cutters

Painting:

Paint pumpkin stem green. **Dry-brush** stem with bright green to lt. yellow. Paint leaves and tendrils with green. Paint stars designated for "W" and "C" magenta. Paint "E" stars aqua. Paint "O" star green. Paint "L" and "M" stars lt. purple. Let dry. Paint miniature stars and lettering black. **Dot** miniature stars with white for eyes. Mix varnish with glitter glaze and brush onto stars as desired.

Decorating:

Beginning with "W" and leaving a 6" length, weave wire down through first hole, behind star, and up through second hole. Curl wire around pencil as desired and repeat process for "E" star. Continue process until all stars are attached, leaving a 6" length at end. Insert ends of wire into pumpkin and bend inside to secure. Hot-glue stars into eyes of pumpkin. Secure stars to top of pumpkin as needed.

Snarling Man

Materials:

Acrylic paints: black, black-green, white
Glue gun and glue sticks
Novelty chain
Rhinestones: (3)

Painting:

Mix black-green and white paints and wash over face of pumpkin, making edges darker. Dry thoroughly. Paint and detail pumpkin face referring to pattern.

Decorating:

Hot-glue rhinestones to pupils and one tooth. Wrap and drape chain around stem of pumpkin.

Turkey Candle Holder

Materials:

Pumpkin candle holder: wooden
Acrylic paints: black, brown, dk. brown, med. brown, copper, gold, iridescent green, smoked pearl, dusty pink, lt. pink, red, dk. red, yellow, dk. yellow, lt. yellow, med. yellow, white
Candle: 8"
Flow medium
Glaze: clear
Sealer: all-purpose
Sponge: small silk

Painting:

Mix all-purpose sealer with black paint. Mix glaze and flow medium 1:1 and moisten candle with sponge. Sparsley **sponge** copper. Using same sponge without rinsing, **sponge** with lesser amount of gold. Rinse sponge. Sparsely **sponge** iridescent green. Thin iridescent green with flow medium and drip along top of candle. Referring to pattern and General Instructions, paint and detail turkey as follows: **base**–body med. brown; eyes white; irises brown; pupils black; beak med. yellow; gobbler red; **float** (shade)–feathers and outer body dk. brown; eyes med. brown; beak dk. yellow; gobbler dk. red; **float** (highlight)–tips of feathers and entire top edge of wings smoked pearl; beak lt. yellow; gobbler dusty pink; **line**–eyebrows, eyelashes, eyes, beak, gobbler, body, feathers and legs black; feathers and feet smoked pearl; **comma strokes**–beak white; gobbler lt. pink. Place candle in candle holder.

Gray Guy

Materials:

Acrylic paints: black, charcoal, white
Glue gun and glue sticks
Novelty items: black spider, large; spider web
Straight pins

Painting:

Mix charcoal and white with equal amounts of water over face of pumpkin. Let dry thoroughly. Paint and detail pumpkin, referring to pattern.

Decorating:

Hot-glue spider to forehead. Pull and stretch spider web around pumpkin. Secure with pins.

Monster

Materials:

Hubbard squash
Acrylic paints: black, dk. green, magenta, orange, lt. pink, lt. purple, dk. red, white
Bolts: 3" metal (2)
Glue gun and glue sticks
Mop cord: 5 yds
Spray bottle

Painting:

Thin dk. red with water in spray bottle. Spray paint mop cord. Thin magenta paint with water and apply to face of squash. Referring to pattern and General Instructions, paint and detail face as follows: **base**–eyes white; irises dk. green; pupils black; eyebrows orange; cheeks and nose lt. pink; **float** (shade)–eyes lt. purple; cheeks magenta; **float** (highlight)–cheeks, nose and mouth lt. pink; **line**–eyelashes, small strokes in eyebrows, eyes, nose, and mouth black; **comma strokes**–cheeks, nose and mouth white; **dots**–eyes, cheeks and nose white.

Decorating:

Cut mop cord into 8" lengths. Hot-glue to top of squash. Insert bolts into side of squash, referring to photograph for placement.

"Toadal" Spell

Materials:

Pumpkin: compressed styrofoam
Acrylic paints: black, brown, lt. brown lt. gray, green, bright green, dk. green, magenta, dk. pink, dk. purple, bright red, dk. red, white, lt. yellow
Balls: wooden 3/4" (2 for eyes)
Crackle medium
Egg: 2 1/2" wooden (cut in half for body)
Glaze: glitter
Craft glue
Ribbon: 1/4"-wide lavender silk, 12"
Varnish: clear

Painting:

Base-coat pumpkin with dk. purple. Apply crackle following manufacturer's instructions. Mix bright red and lt. yellow 1:1. Paint as overcoat. **Dry-brush** with dk. red and lt. yellow. Paint stem green. **Dry-brush** stem using bright green to lt. yellow. Glue eyes to body to form toad. Glue toad to pumpkin. Referring to pattern and General Instructions, paint and detail toad as follows: **base**–body, legs and feet green (while paint is still damp, stroke legs and feet with lt. green); eyes white; irises brown; pupils black; spots dk. pink; **float** (shade)–mouth dk.

green; outer spots magenta; **float** (highlight)–irises lt. brown; mouth lt. green; **stipple**–top of eyes and lids lt. gray; cheeks magenta then lt. pink; center of large spots lt. pink; **line**–eyelashes, eyes and mouth black; legs and large spots dk. green; **comma strokes**–pupils white; nose black; additional highlights in legs and feet lt. green; **dots**–white. Mix varnish with glitter glaze and brush onto toad as desired.

Decorating:

Tie ribbon into bow. Glue in place at right side of toad. Mix glitter varnish with glaze. Apply to inside edge of face on pumpkin and on toad.

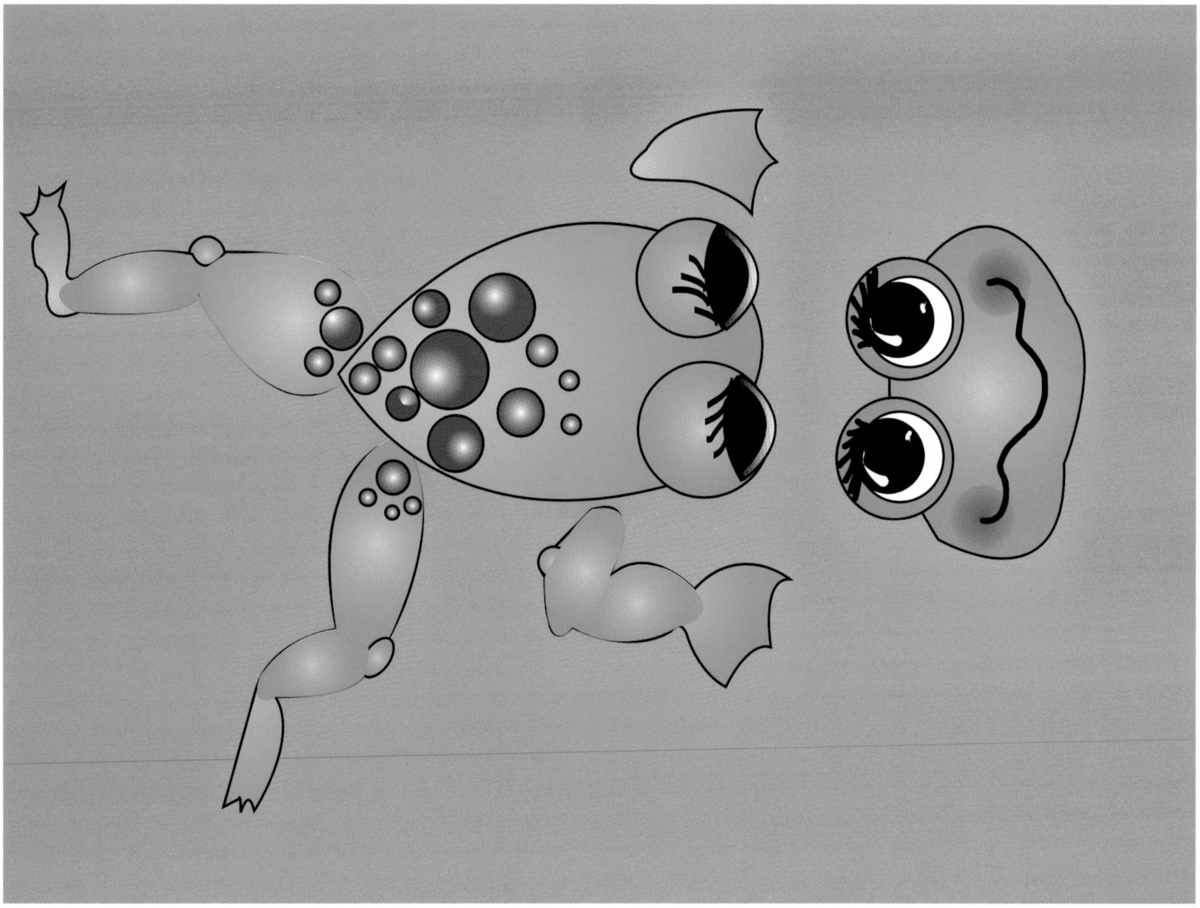

Haunting

Materials:

Acrylic paints: black, dusty blue, brown, magenta, smoked pearl, purple, lt. purple, dk. red, white

Dowel: 1/4"-wide x 8"

Glue gun and glue sticks

Varnish: gloss

Watercolor paper: 4 1/2" x 4 1/2", 400 lb cold-pressed, white

Painting:

Referring to pattern and General Instructions, paint and detail sign on smooth side of watercolor paper as follows: **base**–entire sign brown; **float** (shade)–entire sign black to create wood appearance and dry-brush with smoked pearl; **line**–lettering black; outline lettering smoked pearl; "X", underline and "!" lt. purple; **spatter**–entire sign black and lt. purple. Apply a coat of varnish to both sides of paper.

Paint and detail pumpkin face as follows:

Base–eyes white; irises dusty blue; pupils and "BOO" black; nose magenta; 3-D lettering magenta; **float** (shade)–eyes magenta; nose purple; **stipple**–cheeks dk. red; **line**–eyebrows, eyelashes and nose black; outer lettering magenta; inside lettering dusty blue; **comma strokes**–eyes and nose white; **dots**–eyes white.

Decorating:

Hot-glue paper sign to dowel. Hot-glue dowel to back of pumpkin.

BOO

NO
Hauntin'

Witch Hazel

Materials:

Acrylic paints: black, lt. green, dk. green, white
Novelty items: witch's nose; witch's wig
Straight pins
Witch's hat

Painting:

Paint pumpkin dk. green. Paint and detail pumpkin face, referring to pattern.

Decorating:

Attach wig, hat and nose to pumpkin with straight pins.

Golden Pumpkin

Materials:

Acrylic paints: metallic gold, dk. green
Bronzing powder: antique French
Gold leafing sheets: 1 pkg
Autumn leaf: large
Spray adhesive: industrial-strength

Decorating:

Spray entire pumpkin with spray adhesive. Allow adhesive to set for 1–2 hours. Lay non-shiny side of gold leaf sheet on pumpkin. Rub sheet with fingers and remove sheet. Gold leafing will transfer onto pumpkin. Repeat process, overlapping leafing, until entire pumpkin is covered. Lightly brush bronzing powder over entire pumpkin, excluding stem. Lightly paint random areas of leaf with metallic gold. Hot-glue leaf to base of stem.

Painting:

Mix acrylic paints together 1:1 and paint stem, after all decorating is complete.

Gold Leaf Pumpkin

Materials:

Papier mâché basket: pumpkin-shaped with handle
Acrylic paints: black, brown, burgundy
Brush: soft bristle
Cloth: soft, white
Floral pick: berries
Glue gun and glue sticks
Gold leaf adhesive
Gold leaf sheets (1 package)
Leaves: autumn silk, separated (14)
Retarder
Ribbon: brown ombré wire-edge, 3 yds
Sealer: all-purpose
Spray paint: copper, gold

Painting:

Base-coat pumpkin basket with burgundy. Apply sealer to leaves with soft bristly brush. Brush under and on top of leaves, overlapping to cover papier mâché base. Let some leaves overlap above edge. Let dry thoroughly. Apply gold leaf adhesive to pumpkin according to manufacturer's instructions. Let dry until clear. Apply sheets of gold leaf, overlapping to ensure coverage. Let dry completely before using a soft cloth to rub and remove overlap and excess. Mix brown, black and burgundy 3:1:1 with retarder to consistency of whipping cream. Brush over surface, being certain to apply to detail. Wipe with a small absorbent rag to remove excess. Wipe in one direction. Let dry thoroughly. Apply sealer. Lightly spray seven leaves with copper than gold paint.

Decorating:

Tie ribbon into a four-loop bow with 24" tails. Arrange and hot-glue leaves, bow and berries to left side of basket and handle, referring to photograph for placement. Weave ribbon tails around leaves and handle as desired. Hot-glue ribbon ends to basket.

Silver Pumpkin

Materials:

Acrylic paints: metallic gold, dk. green
Glitter: 7 oz. tubes: gold, iridescent, white opaque
Craft glue
Glue gun and glue sticks
Mixing bowls
Newspaper
Rhinestones: 3/4" clear oval (4–5)
Ribbon: 1 1/2"-wide sheer white with gold edging, 3 1/2 yds; 1 3/8"-wide antique gold wire-edge, 3 yds
Spray paint: gold
Trim: 5/8"-wide white with gold edging, 5 yds

Painting:

Spray entire pumpkin gold. Mix acrylic paints together 1:1 and paint stem.

Decorating:

Mix the three tubes of glitter together. Slightly dilute craft glue with water. Lay pumpkin on its side on newspaper. Using fingers, cover one side of pumpkin with glue. Sprinkle glitter onto pumpkin, gently pressing glitter into glue. Carefully turn pumpkin over and repeat process until entire pumpkin is covered. Set pumpkin upright and allow glue to dry thoroughly. Cut wire-edge ribbon into file 6"–8" lengths and seven 7"–12" lengths. Fold set of five ribbons in half sideways so inner edges touch. Shape folded ends of ribbons into points. Gently gather inner edge wires to form leaves. Twist wires around raw ends and turn under. Using both hands, twist set of seven ribbons until ribbon twists into itself to form tendrils. Cut trim into appropriate lengths to vertically fit around pumpkin. Glue trim to pumpkin. Hot-glue leaves and tendrils around stem of pumpkin. Glue rhinestones to several leaf tips and on pumpkin as desired. Make a multi-looped bow from sheer ribbon and hot-glue around stem and in between leaves and tendrils.

Scary Scenes for Halloween

We enjoy making our homes comfortable and inviting for family and friends. But once a year we rebel and mischievously turn our innocent homes into terrifying, creepy places. Our imaginations run wild, as we offer goodies and tricks to those who dare haunt our doorstep.

Bugs & Hisses

Materials:

Aluminum screen, 6" square
Black acrylic paint
Canning jar with ring
Chocolate candy kisses
Paper tag with black string
Plastic bugs, snake, spiders

Tools:

Black felt-tip marker
Foam brush
Matches

1. Paint canning ring with black acrylic paint, using foam brush. Brush sides of jar with black acrylic paint.

2. Fill jar with chocolate kisses, and plastic bugs and spiders.

3. Write on paper tag: "Hugs and Kisses—Bugs and Hisses," using black felt-tip marker.

4. Burn edges of tag, using matches. Do not let burn more than 2–3 seconds. Tie tag around jar with black string.

5. Place screen square on top of jar and secure with black canning ring. Wrap plastic snake around jar.

TIP: A plastic mummy case can be used in place of a canning jar. After candy is gone, the Bugs & Hisses jar makes a "nice" bug collector.

Scary Treat Bucket

Materials:

Black spray paint
Brown acrylic paint
Candy
Red nail polish
Small galvanized bucket

Tools:

Latex gloves

1. Spray bucket with black spray paint, letting some silver show through. Let dry.

2. Apply brown acrylic paint on one palm of latex-gloved hands. Rub hands together, then gently pat bucket.

3. Drizzle red nail polish down sides.

4. Fill bucket with candy.

TIP: To use the Scary Treat Bucket as a Halloween centerpiece, fill bucket with tomato soup (for decorative effect) and plastic bones. Add dry ice for added effect.

HUGS and Kisses
xoxoxo
BUGS and Hisses

Witch Hat

Materials:

Black tulle ribbon
Bubble wrap
Chicken wire
Raw sienna acrylic paint
Witch hat

Tools:

Craft scissors
Hot-glue gun & glue sticks
Matches
Paintbrush

1. Stuff hat with bubble wrap.

2. Refer to Witch Hat Diagram 1. Cut chicken wire to fit around base of hat, using craft scissors.

3. Burn holes in black ribbon, using matches.

4. Weave black tulle ribbon in and out of chicken wire. Leave ends long enough to tie around hat.

5. Refer to Witch Hat Diagram 2. Adhere woven ribbons to hat, using hot-glue gun.

6. Brush patches randomly around hat with raw sienna acrylic paint, using paintbrush.

Witch Hat Diagram 1

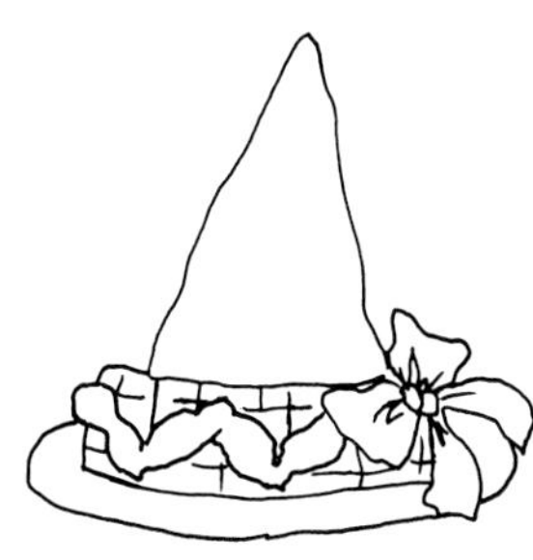

Witch Hat Diagram 2

Broomstick

Materials:

Acrylic paints: black, orange
Black plastic spider
Black sheer nylon ribbon (36")
Black spray paint
Black tulle ribbon (36")
Broom

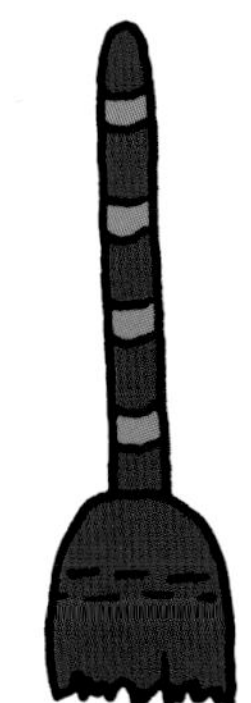

Broomstick Diagram

Tools:

Foam brush
Hot-glue gun & glue sticks
Latex gloves
Masking tape, 2" wide
Matches

1. Paint entire broom with black spray paint. Let dry.

2. Refer to Broomstick Diagram. Wrap strips of masking tape around broom handle every two inches.

3. Paint open sections on handle with orange acrylic paint, using foam brush. Let dry; remove tape.

4. Apply black acrylic paint on one palm of latex-gloved hands. Rub hands together, then gently pat broom handle.

5. Tie black ribbons to lower end of broom handle.

6. Burn holes in ribbon, using matches. Refer to photo on page 110 for placement.

7. Adhere plastic spider to ribbon, using hot-glue gun.

TIP: A spiderweb draped over the Broomstick can add a scary Halloween effect.

Witch Shoes

Pictured on page 110

Materials:

Black rust-preventive spray paint
Black tulle ribbon
Air-dry modeling clay
Old shoes
Paper cups, 8 oz. (2)

Tools:

Craft scissors
Hot-glue gun & glue sticks

1. Cut off rims of paper cups, using craft scissors.

2. Refer to Witch Shoes Diagram 1. Adhere paper cup to toe of each shoe, using hot-glue gun.

3. Form modeling clay around cup until smooth to make long, pointed toes. Let dry for three days.

4. Refer to Witch Shoes Diagram 2. Remove shoelaces from shoes. Create squiggles randomly around outside of shoes to add texture, using hot-glue gun.

5. Spray shoes with black spray paint.

6. Lace shoes with black tulle ribbon.

"Designer" witch shoes can be a Halloween color other than black.

Witch Shoes Diagram 1

Witch Shoes Diagram 2

Melted Witch

Materials:

Black cloth
Witch hat
Striped socks
Newspaper
Pointy shoes
Broom
Bucket
Dry ice

1. Lay black cloth in a heap on the ground. Place witch hat on top of heap. Stuff striped socks with newspaper and place in pointy shoes. Place socks under fabric like they are just snaking out, ready to trip anyone who passes too close.

2. Burn the straw tips of an old broom. Cut or break the handle end off to about 2 1/2'. Set a bucket on its side next to the heap.

3. A piece or two of dry ice under the hat brim will add the final touch.

The witch pictured on page 113 has melted in front of a decorative sculpture.

Black Moss Chair

Materials:

Black spray paint
Old chair
Spanish moss

Tools:

Hot-glue gun & glue sticks
Leather gloves

1. Adhere Spanish moss sporadically over chair, especially in spots that have been worn, wearing leather gloves and using hot-glue gun.

2. Spray chair with 3–4 coats of black spray paint, covering moss and chair.

3. Place Invisible Man in chair or fill chair with pumpkins, a black cat, or trick or treat buckets filled with candy.

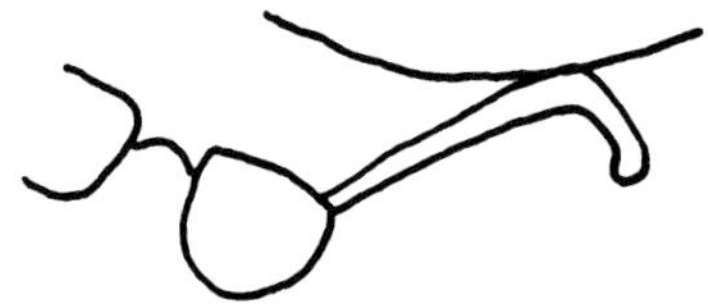

Invisible Man Diagram

Invisible Man

Materials:

Chair
Chrome-colored enamel spray paint
Fishing line or heavy-gauge wire
Glasses
Hat

Tools:

Hot-glue gun & glue sticks

1. Spray hat and glasses with 2–3 coats of chrome-colored spray paint. After all coats, let dry completely.

2. Refer to Invisible Man Diagram above. Adhere glasses to hat at an angle, using hot-glue gun, to suggest someone is wearing them. Spray paint over glued area.

3. Using heavy-gauge wire, secure invisible man to a chair; OR, using fishing line, suspend invisible man from ceiling.

Photo Wreath

Materials:

Black acrylic paint
Black sheer nylon ribbon
Black spray paint
Color copies of Halloween photographs of family and friends
Laminate sheets
Grapevine wreath
Spiders
Spiderweb
White burlap ribbon
White tulle ribbon

Tools:

Hot-glue gun & glue sticks
Latex gloves
Matches
Paper hole punch

1. Spray wreath with black spray paint.

2. Cover color copies of photographs with laminate sheets. Make a small hole at the top of each photo, using paper hole punch.

3. Burn around edges of each photograph copy, using matches. Burn holes in black nylon ribbon and white tulle ribbon.

4. String black ribbon through paper-punched holes and attach photographs to wreath.

5. Make large bows with white tulle and white burlap ribbons.

6. Adhere bows, spiders, and spiderweb to wreath, using hot-glue gun.

7. Apply black acrylic paint on one palm of latex-gloved hands. Rub hands together and gently pat white ribbons.

Tip: The photo wreath can go on the front door— so all of last year's trick-or-treaters can see themselves in costume from the previous year. You may choose to take the photo of a child off the wreath and give it to him or her when coming to visit you.

Spirit Tissues

Materials:

White tissue paper

1. Enlarge Large Ghost and Small Ghost patterns as needed. Cut out several ghosts from tissue paper, making different shapes, positions, and sizes.

2. Take one ghost at a time and wad up paper as tightly as possible.

3. Smooth out paper and tape to mirrors and windows.

LARGE GHOST

SMALL GHOST

Wary Windows

With things found around your house, decorate your most prominent windows. Using thumbtacks, tack old, dusty lace around the window frame. Drape tattered strips of fabric around window corners. Tangle together string and yarn and loop it around the window. Tack Christmas lights around the window and cover with pieces of batting. Hang Dem-Dough-Bones (page 118) in corners or use them for tiebacks. Arrange Spirit Tissues (facing page) so as to peek out from corners or come up from windowsills. String artificial spiderwebs around window corners.

Foreboding Dough

Materials

2 cups flour
1 cup salt
2 tablespoons cooking oil
1 1/4 cup water
paper clip
knitting needle
spray varnish

1. Mix ingredients. Knead into dough.

2. Use cookie cutters or sculpt into desired shapes.

3. Either insert paper clip into top to hang, or poke hole through shape with knitting needles to string. Let dry.

4. Paint with acrylics and spray varnish.

To create dough bats, use a bat-shaped cookie cutter, and paint black when dry. Attach two small red pom-poms for eyes. String ribbon through hole to hang.

Dem-Dough-Bones

Materials

Acrylic paints: black, white
Assorted beads with large holes
Butter knife
Foreboding Dough
Metal knitting needles (2)
Oven
Paint Brush
Pencil
Ribbons or yarns (2–3 yds each color)

1. Pinch off golf-ball-sized pieces of dough, keeping fingers moist and storing remaining dough in airtight container. When smoothing dough or attaching pieces together, use a drop of water. Shape dough into skull shapes.

2. Push skull shapes onto knitting needle. Using butter knife, make facial features and teeth. Using pencil tip, make eye sockets. Continue making skulls until the desired number of odd skulls are on knitting needle.

3. Use similar process to make even number of bones on another knitting needle.

4. Bake skulls and bones at 250° F until hard.

5. When hard and cool, remove from knitting needles. Paint skulls and bones white or leave natural. Paint eye sockets and nose black.

6. Alternately thread bones and skulls onto several lengths of colored ribbon or yarn with knots, adding assorted beads to decorate.

Bat-a-Bat Piñata

Materials

Acrylic paints: black, red, white
Cardboard
Craft knife
Fishing line
Hot-glue gun & glue sticks
Long stick
Masking tape
Paintbrushes
Papier mâché body
Red ribbon
Red tulle squares, 8" x 8"
Small toys
Table-tennis ball
Wrapped candy

1. Cut wings from cardboard. Cut 1" slits into edge of wings that will go next to body. Turn body upside down and tape wings in place. Poke holes in tips of wings to string fishing line for hanging.

2. Paint entire bat black. Cut table-tennis ball in half and hot-glue to body for eyes. Paint red dots on eyes with a black dot in center for dilated pupils. Paint white pointy teeth. Add drops of blood down chin with red paint.

3. Place small toys and wrapped candy in red tulle squares, then secure bundles with ribbon. Place bundles in body and seal with tape to create piñata. Hang piñata low enough for child to hit with stick. Let blind-folded children (or adults) take turns hitting the piñata to break it open.

Scary Tip:

Refer to page 118 to create Dough Bats shown below. String together with ribbon and hang conspicuously around your yard.

Papier Mâché body

Inflate balloon. Mix fabric starch, flour, wallpaper paste, or wheat paste with water until desired consistency for paste. Tear newspaper into strips. Dip strips, one at a time, into mixture, and then run between fingers to eliminate excess. Cover entire balloon with strips. Leave small opening around knot. Hang and let dry. Repeat with more newspaper. Let dry. Pop and remove balloon. Cover again with torn strips of white paper. Let dry.

Spiderweb Invitations

Materials:

Black construction paper, 8 1/2" x 11"
Black jewelry thread
Black rust-preventive spray paint
Halloween-printed clear cellophane
Spider confetti
Spiderweb
Spray adhesive
White copy paper, 8 1/2" x 11"
White high quality paper
White mailing tube
White, marbled translucent paper, 8 1/2" x 11"

Tools:

Black felt-tip marker
Clipboard
Matches
Needle

1. Find an actual, incredible spiderweb outdoors without the spider. Spray web with black spray paint.

2. Place quality paper on clipboard. Spray paper with adhesive spray. Place paper behind web and gently scoop web forward to attach to paper.

3. Size web to fit 8 1/2" x 11" paper. Copy web onto translucent paper.

4. Write party invitation on white 8 1/2" x 11" copy paper, using black felt-tip marker.

5. Burn around edges of translucent copy of web, copy paper with invitation, and black construction paper, using matches.

6. Layer translucent, white, and black papers. Refer to photo on page 122 for placement. Secure layers in top left-hand corner with 4–5 spaced stitches, using needle and thread.

7. Scorch around mailing tube, using matches. Place invitation in mailing tube, along with some spider confetti.

8. Spray tube with adhesive. Cut printed cellophane to fit. Pull cellophane tightly around tube to seal. Mail invitation.

TIP: A spooky face could be substituted for the spiderweb.

Spider Tablecloth

Materials:

Netting or tulle, size of table with 12" overhang
2" Plastic spiders

Tools:

Fabric scissors
Needle & thread
Table

1. Hem netting, using needle and thread.

2. Place netting on table, then place settings on table.

3. Insert each spider's legs into holes of netting until table is overrun with spiders.

TIP: Leftover netting can be made into ghosts and hung in corners.

Black Mask Candle

Materials:

Black mask
Black, oil-based spray paint
Candleholder
Water
White candle

Tools:

Bucket
Hot-glue gun & glue sticks
Latex gloves

Black Mask Candle Diagram

1. Fill bucket with water—enough to submerge entire candle. Spray top of water with three or four squirts of black spray paint.

2. Refer to Black Mask Candle Diagram. Completely immerse white candle upside down in water and paint mixture, using latex-gloved hands.

3. Pull candle out and let dry upright.

4. Paint candleholder with black spray paint. Let dry.

5. Adhere candle into candleholder, using hot-glue gun. Be careful not to melt candle.

6. Place black mask around candle. Pull string tight and tie to secure.

Dripping Candles

Materials:

Candleholder
Household wax, 16 oz.
Spanish moss
White spray paint
White tapered candles (5)

Tools:

Latex gloves
Matches
Measuring cup
Newspaper
Old crockpot

1. Melt household wax in crockpot. Let cool about 20 minutes after melting.

2. Place Spanish moss on newspaper and spray with white spray paint.

3. Place candles in candleholder. Place candleholder on newspaper. Light candles, using matches, and let burn for 5 minutes.

4. Drape Spanish moss around candleholder.

5. Measure out 1/2 cup of melted wax, wearing latex gloves. Slowly drip wax at top of candle (do not cover wick) and over Spanish moss. Repeat until desired effect is achieved. Be certain to pour wax slowly. The drips collect better when you pour slowly.

Spiderweb Art

Materials:

Adhesive spray
Black mat for framing
Black rust-preventive spray paint
Frame
High quality paper
Spiderweb
Spray adhesive

Tools:

Clipboard

1. Find an actual, incredible spiderweb—without the spider.

2. Spray spiderweb with black spray paint.

3. Place high quality paper on clipboard. Spray paper with spray adhesive.

4. Place paper behind spiderweb and gently scoop spiderweb forward to attach to paper.

5. Mat and frame spiderweb.

TIP: A broken window could be used as the frame for Spiderweb Art.

Spiderweb Diagram

Spiderweb Glass

Materials:

Wine glass

Tools:

Masking tape
White accent pen

1. Tape copy of Spiderweb Pattern on facing page to inside of glass.

2. Trace over pattern on outside of glass with white accent pen.

3. Remove pattern.

Spider Ice Cubes

Materials:

Dish soap
Rubber spiders (16)
Water

Tools:

Freezer
Ice cube tray

1. Clean rubber spiders with dish soap in warm water; rinse well. Place spider in each section of ice cube tray.

2. Cover each spider with water. Make certain a spider remains in each tray section. Place ice cube tray in freezer and allow cubes to freeze solid.

TIP: If using ice cubes in drinks, please remind child guests that spiders should not be swallowed!

Black Charger

Pictured on page 138

Materials:

Black "chalkboard" spray paint
White chalk
Wooden chargers (one for each guest)

1. Spray chargers with 3–4 coats black spray paint. Let dry.

2. Write a Halloween message on each charger with white chalk.

TIP: Scary pictures can be drawn on Black Charger, rather than a written message.

Bat Napkin

Materials:

Black square cloth napkin
Pipe cleaners (3)

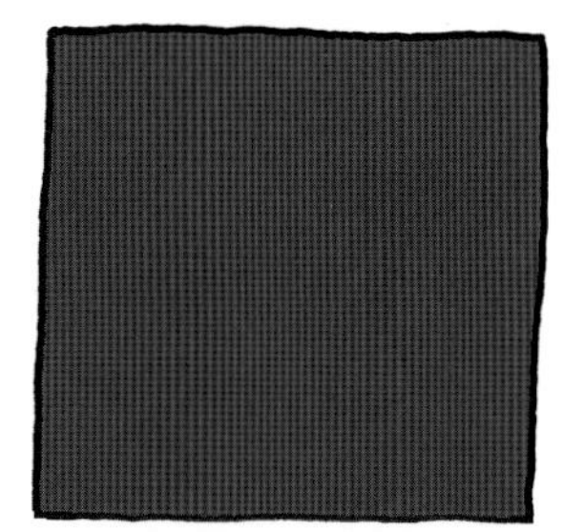

1. Fold dinner napkin into quarters.

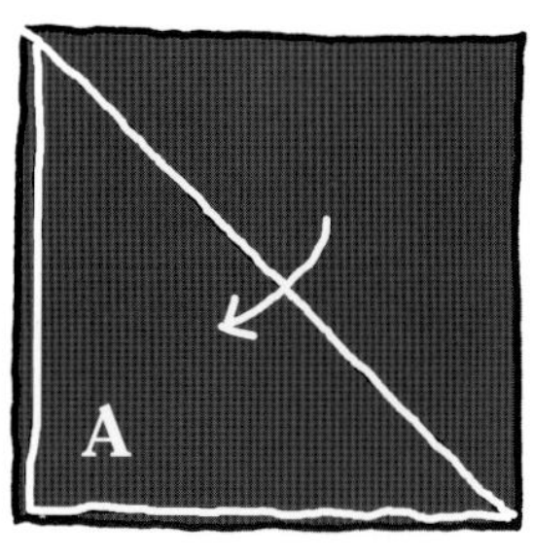

2. Fold back first flap (A).

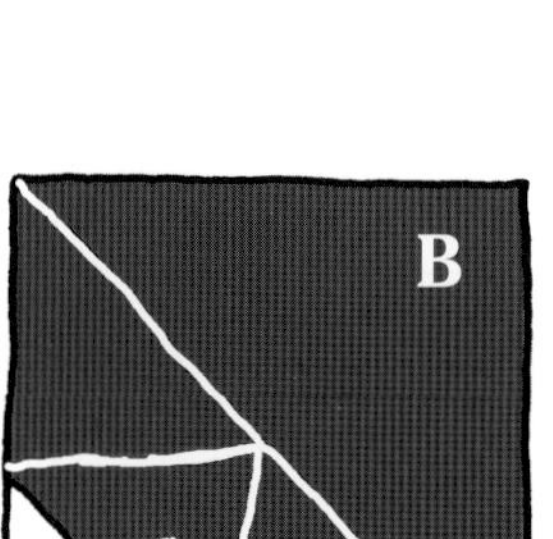

3. Fold point A back to center.

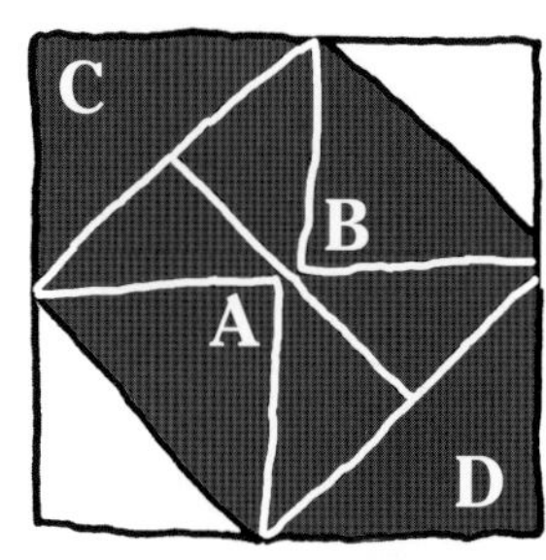

4. Fold second flap (B) to center.

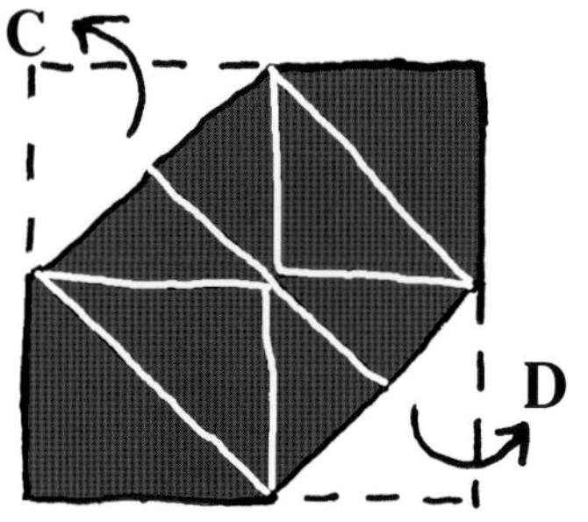

5. Fold C & D toward back to meet in center of back.

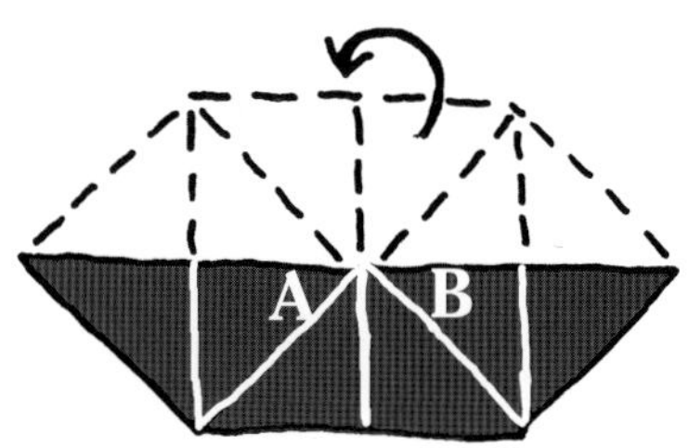

6. Fold napkin in half with A & B on top.

7. Place edges on bottom. Squeeze and wrap center with pipe cleaner. Twist to secure.

8. Fold pipe cleaner in center, then in quarters to create bat ears. Repeat with another pipe cleaner.

9. Twist both pipe cleaners together.

10. Repeat steps 8 and 9 on other side of bat ear.

Richard

Cyclopes Mug

Materials:

Black decorating frosting
Fruit-chew candies
Mug
Roll candies
White frosting

Tools:

Butter knife

1. Dab white frosting on roll candies, using butter knife. Then attach to mug. Dab frosting on fruit-chew candy and attach to roll candies. Refer to Cyclopes Mug Diagram. Dot eye with black decorating frosting.

2. Repeat this process until mug is randomly covered.

Cyclopes Mug Diagram

Flowerpot Place Card

Pictured on page 129

Materials:

Black, oil-based spray paint
Dowel, 1/8"-dia. (8" long)
Name tag
Spanish moss
Styrofoam ball, 2 1/2"-dia.
Terra cotta pot, 2 1/2"-dia.
White flower pick

Tools:

Black felt-tip marker
Craft glue
Hot-glue gun & glue sticks
Matches

1. Adhere styrofoam inside pot, using craft glue.

2. Adhere small amount of Spanish moss to styrofoam.

3. Insert dowel and stem of pick into styrofoam. Spray dowel, pick, and pot with black spray paint.

4. Write name on tag, using black felt-tip marker. Burn edges of tag, using matches.

5. Adhere name tag to dowel, using hot-glue gun.

TIP: Another interesting place card can be made to represent a tombstone with the guest's name incorporated in the epitaph.

Witch Hat Place Card

Materials:

Black, oil-based spray paint
Black pipe cleaner
Black raffia
Black ribbon (6" long)
Decorative cupcake liner
Green pepper
Green plastic eyes, 3/4", (1 pair)
Heavyweight place card
Paper cup, 8 oz.
Small rubber spider
Small witch hat
White tulle, 6" square

Tools:

Black felt-tip marker
Craft scissors
Hot-glue gun & glue sticks
Nail
Ruler

1. Make hole in tip of witch hat, using nail.

2. Refer to Witch Hat Place Card Diagram 1 on page 132. Tie a knot in one end of pipe cleaner and push untied end up through hole from inside hat.

3. Apply hot-glue to knot, using hot-glue gun, and pull pipe cleaner up and tight, adhering knotted pipe cleaner to inside of hat.

4. Cut tulle into a circle. Cut 1/4"-dia. hole in center of tulle.

5. Refer to Witch Hat Place Card Diagram 2 on page 132. Place tulle over hat, stringing pipe

cleaner through hole. Refer to photo on page 133 for placement. Tie black ribbon around base of hat, securing tulle. Trim tulle edges around hat, using craft scissors.

6. Cut black raffia into 12" strands, using craft scissors. Bundle strands together. Tie bundle into knot close to one end, leaving enough length to create short bangs for witch's hair. Trim front raffia to create bangs.

7. Adhere knotted raffia around inside rim of hat, using hot-glue gun.

8. Adhere hat with hair to green pepper. Sometimes a green pepper will stand up better when turned upside down.

9. Carefully push green plastic eyes through front of green pepper.

10. Fill paper cup with water. Spray one or two squirts of black spray paint in cup of water.

11. Dip entire place card into cup of water, pull out, and let dry.

12. Handwrite guest's name on place card in a squiggle print (for a scary effect), using black felt-tip marker.

13. Refer to Witch Hat Place Card Diagram 3. Adhere printed place card to back of spider, using hot-glue gun. Adhere spider and card to end of pipe cleaner.

14. Place witch's head on a flattened, decorative cupcake liner.

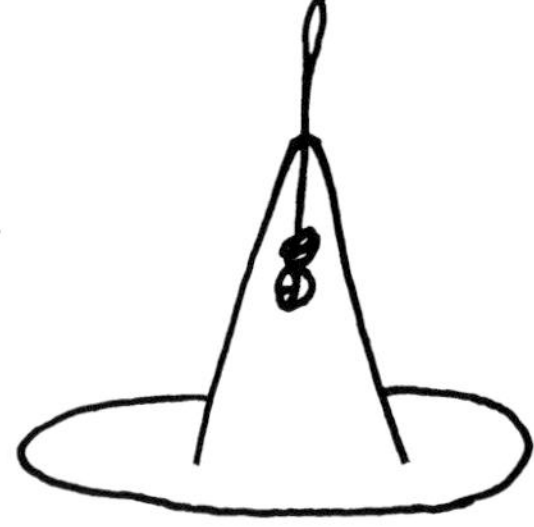

Diagram 1

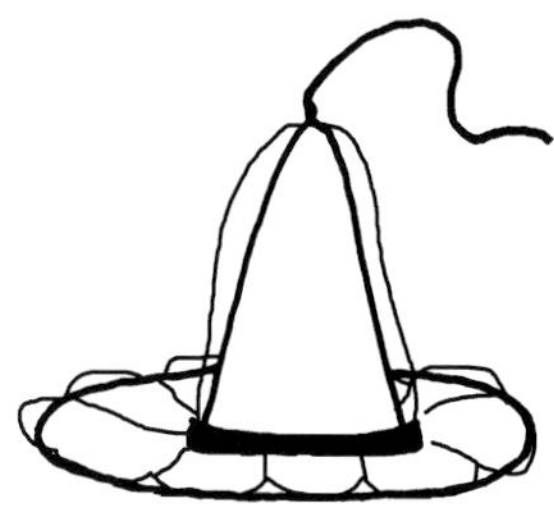

Diagram 2

Diagram 3

Candy Corn Candle Pot

Diagram 1

Diagram 2

Materials:

Acrylic paints: orange, white, yellow
Candy corn
Styrofoam circle, 6"-dia.
Terra cotta pot, 7"-dia.
Yellow candle, 4"-dia. (8" long)

Tools:

Foam brush
Hot-glue gun & glue sticks
Masking tape
Ruler

1. Refer to Candy Corn Candle Pot Diagram 1. Wrap making tape around pot, 2 1/2" up from bottom.

2. Paint bottom of pot with yellow, using foam brush. Paint rim of pot with white. Let dry.

3. Wrap masking tape around top edge of yellow bottom.

4. Paint middle of pot with orange. Let dry.

5. Apply hot glue around rim of Styrofoam circle, using hot-glue gun. Place Styrofoam circle inside pot.

6. Refer to Candy Corn Candle Pot Diagram 2. Center and adhere bottom of candle to top of styrofoam circle.

7. Fill pot with candy corn.

Napkin Candles

Materials:

Black acrylic paint
Découpage medium
Glass jar
Halloween napkin or tissue paper
Orange glitter nail polish
Votive candle

Tools:

Foam brush, $1^{1}/_{2}$"
Latex gloves
Matches

1. Cover outside of jar with découpage medium, using foam brush.

2. If napkin is two-ply, tear outside layer off for a sheer effect.

3. Place napkin or tissue paper around jar; pat down softly. Let dry.

4. Apply découpage medium over outside of jar. Let dry.

5. Apply black acrylic paint on one palm of latex-gloved hands. Rub hands together and gently pat jar.

6. Drizzle black acrylic paint and orange glitter nail polish down sides of jar.

7. Place votive inside jar and light, using matches.

Tip: Drawing a scary picture on the side of the votive candle sends an eerie look into the room when candle is lit.

Richard
Spiders
Witches
Dracula

Halloween Party Recipes

Even though you are all grown up and candy does not hold the allure it once did, Halloween can still make the mouth water. These recipes can make an enjoyable family dinner, or feature in a fabulous Halloween fête. Enjoy!

Roasted Pumpkin Seeds

Pumpkin seeds
Salt
Melted butter (unsalted)
Vegetable oil spray

1. Preheat oven to 350° F.

2. Rinse pumpkin seeds well. For every 2 cups of seeds, place 4 cups of water and 2 tablespoons of salt into a saucepan. Add seeds and simmer over low heat for 10 minutes. Drain well.

3. Place seeds on paper towels and pat dry.

4. For every 2 cups of seeds, toss with 1 tablespoon melted, unsalted butter in a large bowl until seeds are evenly coated. Spray a cookie sheet with vegetable oil spray. Spread seeds on cookie sheet and bake for 30 minutes, stirring and tossing occasionally. Seeds are ready when golden brown.

Clear Drink

Pictured on page 138

Lemon-lime soda
White grape juice

1. Mix equal parts lemon-lime soda and white grape juice.

Mandarin Cream Soda

Pictured on page 130

1 liter cream soda
2 cans mandarin orange slices
1 gallon orange juice

1. Place 3 orange slices in each section of ice cube tray. Cover oranges with orange juice. Freeze until solid.

2. Place 3 orange juice cubes in each glass, then fill with cream soda.

Ghoul-Aid

Photo on page 140.

1 pkg. grape powdered fruit drink
1 pkg. orange powdered fruit drink
3 qts. cold water
2 cups sugar
1 qt. ginger ale

1. Combine both powdered fruit drink flavors in a pitcher and make according to package directions. Add ginger ale and stir to mix well. Pour into a punch bowl and serve over ice. This punch is as black as midnight and is frightfully delicious!

Beefed Up Buns

Pictured at right.

1 1/2 lbs. lean ground beef
1/2 cup chopped onion
1/4 tsp. oregano
1/2 tsp. salt
1/2 tsp. seasoned salt
1/8 tsp. garlic powder
1/2 cup brown sugar
1 tsp. prepared mustard
1 8-oz. can tomato sauce
Hamburger buns
Orange food spray
1 4-oz. pkg. cream cheese
1 tsp. milk
Cake decorating paste, concentrated: black and brown

1. In a large skillet, combine ground beef and chopped onion and cook over medium heat until ground beef is browned. Add next seven ingredients to skillet. Mix well and allow to simmer until hot.

2. Using a sharp knife, remove strips from the top of each hamburger bun. Spray hamburger buns with orange food spray to resemble pumpkins.

3. Mix cream cheese and milk until smooth. Add black cake-decorating paste to mixture for desired color. A hint of brown cake-decorating paste must be added so the black does not turn purple. Place mixture into a frosting bag and, using a cake decorating tip, draw a face on the top of each hamburger bun.

4. Put hot hamburger mixture inside buns and serve.

Cranberry Cider

Pictured at right.

1 pkg. fresh cranberries
2 cinnamon sticks
9 whole cloves
3 qts. water
1 1/2 cup sugar
1/2 cup orange juice
1/4 cup lemon juice

1. Combine first four ingredients in large saucepan. Bring to boil, cover, and simmer for 25 minutes.

2. Strain and discard cranberry pulp, cinnamon sticks, and whole cloves. Immediately add sugar, orange juice, and lemon juice and stir until sugar is dissolved.

3. Pour into a punch bowl and serve hot or allow to cool and serve over ice.

Makes 3 quarts

Creamy Chicken Baked in a Pumpkin

1 small pumpkin
2 lbs. boneless chicken breast, cut into strips
1 can cream of celery soup
1 can cream of chicken soup
1/2 cup sour cream
Salt and pepper to taste
2 tbsp. sesame seeds
1 tbsp. butter
1 bundle green onions, sliced

1. Slice off 1/4 top of pumpkin. Clean out seeds. Save top to use as lid.

2. Brown chicken in pan. Set aside.

3. Sauté sesame seeds and green onions in butter. Take off heat. Add soups, sour cream, and salt and pepper.

4. Pour mixture into cleaned pumpkin. Replace lid and place on baking sheet. Bake at 350° F for 1 1/2 hours. Serve warm. Do not forget to scoop some pumpkin inside with each serving.

*Can be served over bed of pasta.

Dracula's Bow Tie Pasta

Pictured on page 138

12 oz. bow tie pasta
1 tbsp. olive oil
2 cloves garlic, thinly sliced
4 roma tomatoes, peeled and diced
Leaves of 1 bunch fresh basil, thinly sliced
1/3 cup chicken broth
Salt and pepper to taste
3/4 cup freshly grated parmesan cheese

1. Cook bow tie pasta in a large pot of boiling salted water for about 13 minutes.

2. Heat olive oil in medium skillet over medium heat. Sauté garlic until lightly brown.

3. Add tomatoes, basil, and chicken broth. Cook 3 minutes. Sprinkle with salt and pepper.

4. Place pasta in serving bowl and toss with sauce and parmesan cheese

* low fat dish

Dinner In A Pumpkin

Photo on page 140.

Medium-sized pumpkin (4 lbs.)
1 1/2 lbs. lean ground beef
1/3 cup chopped green pepper
3/4 cup chopped celery
3/4 cup chopped onion
1 tsp. salt
1/4 tsp. pepper
1/4 cup soy sauce
2 tbsp. brown sugar
1 4-oz. can mushrooms
1 can cream of chicken soup
2 cups cooked rice
Black olives
1 steamed carrot
Whole cloves
Fresh parsley leaves

1. Using a sharp knife, cut lid from pumpkin and scoop out pumpkin seeds and excess membrane with a scraping tool.

2. In a large skillet, combine ground beef, chopped green pepper, chopped celery, and chopped onion and cook over medium heat until ground beef is browned. Add next seven ingredients to skillet. Mix well and place mixture into pumpkin cavity.

3. Place lid on pumpkin. Place pumpkin on a foil-lined cookie sheet and bake at 350° F for 1 1/2 hours.

4. Just before serving, embellish pumpkin by placing (with toothpicks) black olives to make eyes, a steamed carrot to make a nose, and whole cloves to make a mouth. Use fresh parsley leaves to make hair around lid opening. To serve, scoop out part of the baked pumpkin, along with the meat mixture, onto each plate.

Candy Corn Chowder

5 slices bacon
1 medium onion, thinly sliced
3 medium potatoes, pared and diced
Water
1 box frozen honey-glazed carrots
1 pkg. white sauce mix
1 17-oz. can cream-style corn
1 tsp. salt
Dash pepper

1. In a large frying pan, cook bacon until crisp. Crumble and set aside. Reserve 3 tbsp. bacon drippings in pan.

2. Add onion and cook until light brown. Add potatoes and carrots. Add enough water to cover.

3. Cook over medium heat 10–15 minutes, until potatoes and carrots are cooked.

4. Cook white sauce, following package instructions. Stir in cream-style corn, salt, and pepper. Add to potato and carrot mixture and heat through about 10 minutes.

5. Top each serving with crumbled bacon.

Pumpkin Muffins

3/4 cup packed brown sugar
1/4 cup molasses
1/2 cup soft unsalted butter
1 egg, beaten
1 cup canned pumpkin
1 3/4 cups flour
1 tsp. baking soda
1/4 tsp. salt
1/4 cup chopped pecans

1. In a medium bowl, cream sugar, molasses, and butter. Add eggs and pumpkin and blend well.

2. In another bowl, mix flour with baking soda and salt; then beat into pumpkin mixture. Fold in pecans.

3. Fill well-greased muffin pans half full with batter. Bake at 375° F for 20 minutes.

Makes 16 muffins

Herbed Pumpkin Bowl

1 small, fresh pumpkin
1/4 cup melted butter
Salt, pepper, and thyme to taste

1. Preheat oven to 400°. Cut pumpkin top off. Scrape out seeds and pulp with spoon.

2. Lightly brush pumpkin with melted butter. Sprinkle with salt, pepper, and thyme to taste. Bake for 30–40 minutes until tender.

3. Fill pumpkin with whipped potatoes or favorite soup and serve warm.

Snack-o-Lanterns

3 tbsp. margarine
10-oz. pkg. marshmallows
6 cups crispy rice cereal
Vegetable oil spray
Orange decorating gel

1. Melt margarine in a large saucepan over low heat. Add marshmallows and stir until completely melted. Remove from heat. Add crispy rice cereal and stir until well coated.

2. Coat 13" x 9" x 2" pan with vegetable oil spray and press crispy rice mixture evenly into pan. When mixture has cooled slightly, cut into circles using a 3-inch round cookie cutter. Using orange decorating gel, decorate each treat with a pumpkin face.

Makes 12 Snack-o-Lanterns

Sherbet Jack-o-Lanterns

Fresh oranges
Orange sherbet
Permanent marker, black

1. Cut the top off each fresh orange and remove the pulp from inside each orange using a spoon. Rinse and allow outsides of oranges to dry thoroughly—about 15 minutes.

2. Using a black permanent marker, draw a jack-o-lantern face on each orange. Fill each orange with orange sherbet and place in freezer until sherbet is frozen.

Gelatin Wigglers

Photo on page 143.

6 4-oz. pkgs. gelatin: 2 each of grape, pineapple, and cranberry
Colored candy

1. Make each gelatin flavor separately, according to package directions.

2. When set, cut gelatin into diamond shapes. To remove gelatin diamonds, place pans in hot water for approximately 15 seconds to loosen edges.

3. Arrange gelatin diamonds in a harlequin pattern on a serving platter and place one colored candy between each two gelatin diamonds.

Treats

Pumpkin Bars

2 cups pumpkin
4 eggs, beaten
1 cup oil
2 cups sifted all-purpose flour
1 cup brown sugar
1 cup sugar
1/4 tsp. salt
1 tsp. baking powder
1 tsp. baking soda
1 1/2 tsp. cinnamon
1/2 tsp. cloves
1/2 tsp. nutmeg

1. Blend pumpkin, eggs, and oil in a mixing bowl. Blend all the dry ingredients together, then fold into pumpkin mixture.

2. Pour onto a greased 9" square cake pan. Bake in a preheated 350° F oven for 20–25 minutes.

3. Remove from the oven and cool to room temperature before frosting with Cream Cheese Frosting.

Makes 20 bars

Cream Cheese Frosting

3 oz. cream cheese, softened
1/2 cup butter
1/2 cup powdered sugar
1/2 tsp. vanilla
1 1/2 tsp. light cream

1. Mix cream cheese with butter. Whip in sugar, vanilla, and light cream. Spread over Pumpkin Bars.

Crow Cookies

Photo on page 148.

Crow Cookie Cutter

1 1/2 cup confectioner's sugar
2 1/2 cup flour
1 cup butter or margarine
1 egg
1 tsp. baking soda
1 tsp. vanilla
1 tsp. cream of tartar
1/2 tsp. almond extract
Candy eyes
Black shoelace licorice

1. Combine first eight ingredients together in a large mixing bowl. Stir until thoroughly mixed and refrigerate for 2 to 3 hours.

2. While cookie dough is chilling, make a crow-shaped cookie cutter by tracing Crow Cookie Cutter pattern onto a disposable plastic lid (such as one from a tub of margarine). Cut crow shape out. Using a rolling pin, roll out chilled cookie dough to 1/4" thickness. Dip plastic crow-shaped cookie cutter into flour and place it on top of cookie dough. Using a paring knife, cut around crow shape. Repeat process until all cookie dough has been used. Mold edges of each crow cookie so they are smooth. Using a broken toothpick, poke holes in bottom of crow to accommodate crow's legs.

3. Bake at 375° F for 7 to 8 minutes. Allow cookies to cool and frost.

4. Embellish each crow cookie with candy eyes and use shoelace licorice to make crow's legs. Cut each piece of licorice in half and thread it through holes in bottom of crow.

Frankenstein Cake Cone

Diagram 1

Diagram 2

Black decorating frosting in tube
Candy eyes
Chocolate cake mix
Chocolate frosting
Green ice cream cone, flat-bottomed
Licorice roll candy: black with orange center
Peanut butter cup
Small green candies

1. Prepare chocolate cake mix, following package instructions.

2. Fill ice cream cone 1/2 full of cake batter and bake, following cupcake instructions on package. Let cool.

3. Apply chocolate frosting on top of baked cones, using butter knife.

4. Remove paper from one peanut butter cup and place on top of frosting. Let set.

5. Refer to Diagram 1. Make stitches from top of cone down the "head" at an angle with black frosting.

6. Attach candy eyes and make mouth with black frosting.

7. Attach one small green candy to each side of cone with black frosting. Let set.

8. Refer to Diagram 2. Attach a small slice of licorice roll to green candy with black frosting.

Mom's Pumpkin Pie

4 eggs, slightly beaten
1 can pumpkin pie filling
1 1/2 cups sugar
1 tsp. salt
1 tsp. cinnamon
1/2 tsp. ginger
1/4 tsp. cloves
2 cups milk

1. Mix ingredients in order given and pour mixture into unbaked pie crust.

2. Bake at 425° F for 15 minutes. Reduce oven to 350° F; continue baking for 45 minutes or until knife comes out clean.

Makes two 9" pies

Pie Crust

4 cups sifted all-purpose flour
1 tsp. salt
2 tsp. baking powder
1/2 cup shortening
1/4 cup hot water
1/2 cup butter
1 tsp. lemon juice
1 egg yolk, beaten

1. Sift flour, salt, and baking powder together. Cut in shortening. Combine hot water with butter and lemon juice, then beat in egg yolk. Mix into dry ingredients. Chill. Use as required.

Makes two 9" pies

Chocolate Scaredy Snacks

3 tbsp. margarine
10 oz. pkg. marshmallows
6 cups crispy rice cereal
Vegetable oil spray
1 cup chocolate chips
Orange candy sprinkles

1. Melt margarine in a large saucepan over low heat. Add marshmallows and stir until completely melted. Remove from heat. Add crispy rice cereal and stir until well coated.

2. Using 1/2-cup measuring cup coated with vegetable oil spray, portion warm crispy rice mixture and firmly shape into round balls. Insert a popsicle stick in the center of each ball.

3. Melt chocolate chips in a small saucepan over low heat and dip the bottom of each ball into melted chocolate. Decorate each ball with candy sprinkles. Refrigerate until chocolate is firm.

Makes 12 balls

Cream Crowdie

A *cranachan* or cream crowdie is a traditional Scottish dessert popular on Halloween night, and is used in divination games. When assembling the dessert, the host would insert coins, rings, and marbles into the mix. Those who got a coin would have a prosperous future, those who got a ring would get married, and those who got a marble were destined for a life of loneliness. If nothing was found in the dessert, the future was said to be uncertain. This dessert is sweet and a little bit decadent (note the whiskey) but very easy to make.

6 tbsp. oatmeal
20 oz. double cream
6 tbsp. honey
6 tbsp. single malt whiskey
trinkets to mix into desserts: coins, rings, or marbles
1 pint raspberries or strawberries
parfait glasses

1. Toast the oatmeal until it is golden brown. Let it cool in the pan.

2. Place the cream in a bowl and whisk until soft and relatively thick.

3. Add the honey and single malt whiskey and fold it in with a whisk until it's soft and creamy. If you're planning to add trinkets to the mixture, do it now.

4. Put a few raspberries in the bottom of each parfait glass. Fold the rest into the cream mixture.

5. Spoon the rest of mixture into the glasses, then add cream to the top and sprinkle on the oatmeal. Add a few more raspberries to the top and chill for three hours.

Dirt Dessert

Cream-filled chocolate cookies
Chocolate or vanilla ice cream
Gummy worms

1. Using a butter knife, scrape cream centers from chocolate cookies. Using a rolling pin, roll chocolate cookies into crumbs to make dirt. Place chocolate cookie crumbs into the bottom of each serving dish, reserving some crumbs.

2. Using a large spoon, scoop ice cream from carton and place in serving dishes. Sprinkle reserved cookie crumbs on top of ice cream and place in freezer to set.

3. Just before serving, place gummy worms in the dessert so they appear to be crawling out of the dirt.

Soul Cakes

In eighteenth- and nineteenth-century Ireland and England, women baked soul cakes on October 31 and November 1 in preparation for All Souls' Day, November 2. On All Souls' Day, children went from door to door "souling": singing and begging for soul cakes or, in some areas, exchanging soul cakes for candy or pennies. Later that night, families ate soul cakes after dinner and performed Souling Night plays.

Try making your own soul cakes on All Hallows' Eve using the following recipe.

2 sticks butter
3 3/4 cups sifted flour
1 cup sugar
1/4 teaspoon nutmeg or mace
1 teaspoon each of cinnamon, ginger, and allspice
2 eggs
2 teaspoons malt vinegar or cider vinegar
Powdered sugar

1. Preheat the oven to 350° F.

2. Cut the butter into the flour with a pastry blender or fork.

3. Blend in the sugar, nutmeg, cinnamon, and allspice.

4. Beat the eggs in a separate bowl, then add in the vinegar. Add the egg mixture to the flour mixture and beat until a stiff dough forms.

5. Knead thoroughly and roll out, 1/4 inch thick. Cut the dough into 3-inch rounds and set on a greased baking sheet.

6. Prick the tops of the cakes with a fork. Bake for 20 to 25 minutes. Let cool and sprinkle with powdered sugar.

Champagne Punch

As an elegant addition to your dessert table, try this rich champagne punch recipe.

1 cup orange-flavored liqueur
1 cup brandy
1/2 cup black raspberry liqueur
2 cups unsweetened pineapple juice
1 quart chilled ginger ale
2 chilled 250 oz. bottles dry champagne

1. In a bowl, combine the orange-flavored liqueur, the brandy, the black raspberry liqueur, and the pineapple juice and chill the mixture, covered, for at least 4 hours or overnight.

2. In a large punch bowl, combine the chilled mixture with ginger ale and champagne and add ice cubes.

Makes about 16 cups

Libations

At a Halloween party you may choose to serve your guests the libation most commonly associated with voodoo, the Zombie. You may also want to try another concoction strongly associated with New Orleans and Halloween voodoo magic, the Hurricane. Both are powerful brews, so advise your guests to exercise restraint—a single one of these drinks per guest is a good rule of thumb. You should also provide some options for the non-drinking guest. A delicious Planter's Punch "mocktail" is the perfect choice for this party.

Planter's Punch Mocktail

3 ounces orange juice
1 ounce lime juice
1 teaspoon passion fruit syrup
Dash of grenadine
Dash of Angostura bitters

Blend in an Irish coffee glass or Tom Collins glass. Garnish with an orange slice.

Zombie

1 ounce light rum
1 ounce dark rum
1/4 ounce 151 proof rum
1/2 ounce apricot brandy
1 ounce pineapple juice
1 ounce lime juice
2 ounces orange juice
1 cup crushed ice
1 teaspoon superfine sugar

Shake in a cocktail shaker if you have one. If not, blend with a stirrer or in a blender at low speed. Pour into a Tom Collins glass and garnish with mint sprigs, a cherry, or orange peels. It's acceptable to drink this cocktail with a straw, if desired.

Hurricane Cocktail

1 ounce dark rum
1 ounce light rum
1/2 ounce lime juice
1/2 ounce passion fruit syrup or grenadine

Shake in a cocktail shaker or blend well with a spoon or stirrer. Pour into a big brandy glass and garnish with a lime or orange peels. You can also drink this cocktail with a straw.

Conversion Charts

Inches to Millimetres and Centimetres

Inches	MM	CM	Inches	CM	Inches	CM
1/8	3	0.3	9	22.9	30	76.2
1/4	6	0.6	10	25.4	31	78.7
3/8	10	1.0	11	27.9	32	81.3
1/2	13	1.3	12	30.5	33	83.8
5/8	16	1.6	13	33.0	34	86.4
3/4	19	1.9	14	35.6	35	88.9
7/8	22	2.2	15	38.1	36	91.4
1	25	2.5	16	40.6	37	94.0
1 1/4	32	3.2	17	43.2	38	96.5
1 1/2	38	3.8	18	45.7	39	99.1
1 3/4	44	4.4	19	48.3	40	101.6
2	51	5.1	20	50.8	41	104.1
2 1/2	64	6.4	21	53.3	42	106.7
3	76	7.6	22	55.9	43	109.2
3 1/2	89	8.9	23	58.4	44	111.8
4	102	10.2	24	61.0	45	114.3
4 1/2	114	11.4	25	63.5	46	116.8
5	127	12.7	26	66.0	47	119.4
6	152	15.2	27	68.6	48	121.9
7	178	17.8	28	71.1	49	124.5
8	203	20.3	29	73.7	50	127.0

Yards to Metres

Yards	Metres	Yards	Metres	Yards	Metres	Yards	Metres	Yards	Metres
1/8	0.11	2 1/8	1.94	4 1/8	3.77	6 1/8	5.60	8 1/8	7.43
1/4	0.23	2 1/4	2.06	4 1/4	3.89	6 1/4	5.72	8 1/4	7.54
3/8	0.34	2 3/8	2.17	4 3/8	4.00	6 3/8	5.83	8 3/8	7.66
1/2	0.46	2 1/2	2.29	4 1/2	4.11	6 1/2	5.94	8 1/2	7.77
5/8	0.57	2 5/8	2.40	4 5/8	4.23	6 5/8	6.06	8 5/8	7.89
3/4	0.69	2 3/4	2.51	4 3/4	4.34	6 3/4	6.17	8 3/4	8.00
7/8	0.80	2 7/8	2.63	4 7/8	4.46	6 7/8	6.29	8 7/8	8.12
1	0.91	3	2.74	5	4.57	7	6.40	9	8.23
1 1/8	1.03	3 1/8	2.86	5 1/8	4.69	7 1/8	6.52	9 1/8	8.34
1 1/4	1.14	3 1/4	2.97	5 1/4	4.80	7 1/4	6.63	9 1/4	8.46
1 3/8	1.26	3 3/8	3.09	5 3/8	4.91	7 3/8	6.74	9 3/8	8.57
1 1/2	1.37	3 1/2	3.20	5 1/2	5.03	7 1/2	6.86	9 1/2	8.69
1 5/8	1.49	3 5/8	3.31	5 5/8	5.14	7 5/8	6.97	9 5/8	8.80
1 3/4	1.60	3 3/4	3.43	5 3/4	5.26	7 3/4	7.09	9 3/4	8.92
1 7/8	1.71	3 7/8	3.54	5 7/8	5.37	7 7/8	7.20	9 7/8	9.03
2	1.83	4	3.66	6	5.49	8	7.32	10	9.14

Dry and Liquid Measurements

3 tsp. = 1 tbsp.
4 tbsp. = 1/4 cup
1 tbsp. = 14.79 ml

1 ounce = 28.35 grams
1 pound = 453.59 grams
1 cup = 236.6 ml

1 tbsp. = 1/2 fluid ounce
1 cup = 8 fluid ounces
1 quart = 946.4 ml

Index

INDEX

INDEX

Photography appearing in this book between pages 1-58, 107, 139 , page headers & footers are by Keith Wright.

Photographs appearing in this book on pages 59–105, 113, 116–121, 140, 143, and 148 are by Kevin Dilley for Hazen Photography

Photography appearing in this book on pages 109–110, 114–115, 122–138, & 151 supplied by Chapelle Ltd.

Designs for the Pumpkin Decoration section, pages 59–105 in this book are by Amber Hansen, Kathy Frongner, Phillip Romero, Susan Laws, Kelly Henderson, and Vicki Rhodes